YOUNG WRITERS

WRITE AND SHINE

HAMPSHIRE

First published in Great Britain in 1995 by
POETRY NOW
1-2 Wainman Road, Woodston,
Peterborough, PE2 7BU

HB ISBN 1 85731 570 7
SB ISBN 1 85731 575 8

Foreword

Cock-a-doodle-doo, wakey wakey, write and shine!

Welcome to this selection of poems by young writers from your area. The poems you are about to read express thoughts and feelings on a wide range of themes which are close to the poets' hearts. All the poems in this anthology vary in style, content and subject and we hope that you enjoy reading them as much as we did editing them.

So why don't you start your day with a generous serving of poems drenched in imagination and topped with a sprinkling of emotion.

Sarah Andrew
Editor

CONTENTS

City of Portsmouth Boys' School

Andrew Clifton	28
Stuart Hiles	29
Gary Skipper	29
Scott Mussen	30
Christopher Green	30
Edward Smith	31
Ryan Cathrae	31
Phillip Randall	32
Darren Welch	33
Luke Cronin	34
Richard Poole	35

Cove School

Matthew Burrows	35
Matthew Lippiatt	36

Crestwood Community School

Crystal Hawkhead	36
Bryan Light	37
Ben Goble	38
Katie Wilson	39
Sarah Flitney	40
Clair Firmager	41
Emma Clark	41
Stephanie Murray	42
Helen Wooldridge	43
Steven Hodge	44
Sarah Holt	45
Rachel Rogers	45
Claire Bussey	46
Caroline Babey	47
Melissa Annalls	47
Lisa Robins	48
Jemma Gurney	49
Anna Perry	50
Emily Ball	50
Jamie Brewer	51
Sarah Holt	52
Jenny Smith	53

Havant College

Dave Nicholls 80

Henry Beaufort School

Andrew Brinkman 81
James Rice 82
Stephanie Binks 83
Judith Stephens 83
Mark Holloway 84
Matthew Hall 84
Julie Dunn 85
Katy Rabjohn 85
Joanna Glanville 86
Jason Shiner 86
Julian Rowe 87
Natasha Johnson 87
Sophia Mattia 88
Georgina Hoyland 88
Michael Pearlman 89
Kerry-Megan Birkett 89
Jonathan Eacott 90
Gemma August 91
Colette Hooper 91
Peter Sansom 92
Ann Smith 92
Lorraine Machen 93
Alexa Dugmore 93
Nicholas Hooper 94
Katy Grainger-Allen 95
Rachel Mountifield 95
Jenny Burgin 96
Rachel Neave 97
Matthew Flenley 97

Kitbridge Middle School

Joanne Baillie 98
Rachel Hine 98
Zara Davis 99

Kings' School

Gemma Hayes 99

Dax Windsor 124

Rookwood School

Terri Rotchell 125
Rachel Hoyes 126

Richard Aldworth School

Jaimini Mistry 127
Mark Harris 127
Hayley Pfaff 128
Lauren Smith 129
Mark Leather 129
Karen M A Macklin 130
Jodie Pellett 131
Geraint Perkins 131
Adam Hooker 132
Billy Oliphant 133
Samantha Collins 133
Gemma Pugsley 134
David Leake 134
Stephanie Waldron 135
Emma Paddock 136
Lindsay Day 136
Callie Wood 137
Samantha Wheldon 138
Joanna Riley 139
Lucy Smith 139
Natalie Hills 140
Ben Dawe 141
Sally Williams 142
Marc Lilly 143
Katie Bennett 143
Daniel Bailes 144
Natasha Sturdy 144
Richard Smith 145
Ryan Rambaccussing 146
Natalie Stanton 147

Richard Huish College

Poie-Yun Li 147

Ann-Marie Hickman	169
Joanne Cater	169
Hayley Bevis	170
Jody Kenway	170
Marion Ballard	171
Karen Warrington	171
Donna Lane	172
Erica Andrews	172
Gillian Lye	173
Emma Dodge	173
Nicola King	174
Sarah Lieb	175
Kathryn Smurthwaite	175
Joanne Tonner	176
Joanne Ellis	176
Danielle Naulin	177
Laura Carter	177
Jodene Payne	178
Maxine Dawkins	178
Leanne Pearce	179
Georgina Macey	179
Amy Beard	180
Marie Neale	181
Bonny Clayton	182
Kathryn Whinney	183
Kerry Webb	184
Emma Purkiss	184
Kelly Jacqueline Paddick	185
Lauren Hancock	186
Elaine Thomas	186
Emma Male	187
Kerry O'Brien	187
Katie Chant	188
Emma Parkes	189
Joanne Smith	189
Emma Harley	190
Joanna Webb	190
Joanna Gransden	191

Wildern School

Katie Borrill	261
Nigel Parsons	262
Judith Furnell	263
Jayne Smith	263
Lee Stevens	264
Alex Plant	265
Zabunnassa Noor	266
David Fox	267
Sylvia Powell	268
Heather Agnew	268
Hannah Dudley	269
Claire Brooker	269

FREEDOM

As the sun beats down across my back
It feels like I am trapped in a giant prison.
Hoe cakes and water are all we eat.
The constant picking gradually slows,
But the slash of the white-man's whip continues.
The sweltering heat . . .
Oh I long for freedom!

My bike speeds along the small dirt track,
As a cloud of dust flies up.
The New Forest rushes past,
Like the sweat of my forehead.
I stop by the river for a drink . . .
Oh it's lovely to be free!

Richard Lidstone (12) Applemore Technology College

FREEDOM FOR SLAVES

'What's freedom?' Asked a small slave child.
'It's like soaring free like a bird', I replied.
'Like what?' The child asked confused, but
eager to know.
'Freedom is . . .

>Meeting when we want to meet,
>Eating when we want to eat,
>Walking where we want to walk,
>Talking when we want to talk.

>Flying high and swimming low,
>Walking as far as we want
>to go'.

'I understand now, it must be nice, freedom', sighed
the young slave.
'Yes, someday we will have freedom too'.

Rebecca Clayton (12) Applemore Technology College

DEATH IS A COMMA, NOT A FULL-STOP

Death is like a comma in a sentence.
A pause in time,
A break between two worlds,
A beginning not an end as some believe.

The comma brings a joining of ideas.
Life then the after life,
Death is just the doorway,
A superficial but necessary regulation.

The comma is needed in the sentence.
Like our lives in this world,
But they must be used wisely,
Following the great writer of this world's plan.

A full-stop. The end, but death is not like that.
A conjunction in my life,
Just as a comma,
Is the passage way to the next idea.

Bronwen Evans (14) Brighton Hill Community School

GOING FOR A SKATE

White, crispy crunchy snowflakes
Idly fall down from the sky
Northerly winds freeze over the lakes
Transparent sheets of shiny ice
Everywhere like icing on a Christmas cake
Really good weather for going for a skate.

Michael Burt (13) Brighton Hill Community School

THE STORM OF THE LION

The lightning stokes you,
A lion's paw.
When thunder breaks,
The creature roars.
The rain pours down,
A lashing tail,
The torrent floods,
A stalking male.

And when all is quiet,
The lion waits,
Tensing up, his breath
He bates.

The black clouds chase
Their prey, the light.
And lightning sheets,
The final flight.
The moon peers through,
A blinking eye.
The prey falls down,
The younger wins,
And stars return,
The storm's finished.

Almost.

The lion waits.
His breath, he bates.
And as he dies,
In the sky,
The wind is torn
Between the calm,
And its heart
The storm.

Jennie Hodgson (15) Brighton Hill Community School

I'M A DEVIL ON THE RUN!

Woke up this morning with my shining sun within,
Only God knows where I'm going,
Only my eyes know where I've been.
My mind remembers clearly what happened yesterday,
But it all seems so messed up
I can't understand it anyway.

Some say it's the devil's blood they're squeezing from the vine,
Some say I'm a saviour in these hard and desperate times,
But I'm just a devil on the run to find a better life,
'Cause the other ways there's too much pain time after time,
For I just help them to forget,
That we're just born to die.

I didn't have too good a feeling as I head out to the night,
To find my piece of easy street,
To find my better life,
Where the streets are paved with gold,
Where I can rest my desperate soul.

I know nothing good comes easy,
And all good things take some time,
But across the border they turn water into wine,
And now I've made my bed, I'll lie in it,
Just to die in it's the crime,
And if I could choose the way I'd die,
I'd make it by a gun or knife,
'Cause the other ways there's too much pain,
Time after time.

Christopher Meaden (13) Brighton Hill Community School

4

THE BLITZ

The soft sound of blackbirds singing,
Fills the stuffy air,
The wind plays gently with the fragile,
Branch of the old oak tree,
Casually raindrops fall, drizzling down windows.

Screams fill the air, with frightening warning siren,
Explosion, destroy it aiming target,
People rushing nervously for cover,
As flames dance wickedly behind them.

The eerie silence fills the air,
Men digging to find injured people,
Sighs of relief fill the streets,
As the Blitz dies down.

Laura Shirley (12) Brighton Hill Community School

AUTUMN

As I tossed and turned I could feel
The fresh sense of ice.

I opened my eyes and walked towards
The window,
As I slowly opened it,
I could hear the ice crack and fall
From the window.

The air was cold like snow,
And the leaves were crispy and pretty
As a rainbow.

The sky was as clear as water,
The sense was as fresh as snow.

Natasha Eccott (12) Brighton Hill Community School

NIGHT

The sky gradually fades into darkness,
The sun sinks to the ground,
The protection of light gone,
The invasion of night begins.
A breeze against my face,
A scuttling behind me.
An eerie shudder goes down my spine,
As I sense the night is here.
A welcoming light in the distance,
A place to escape the fear,
Something rushing past my feet,
It is coming near.
The light gives me safety,
But not protection from him,
A wind rushes past me,
Unfortunately time does not.
A startling howl,
An eerie hoot,
A brisk cold wind,

The light,
The final light,
Is out,
And I'm all alone,
With the dark,
Dark,
Night.

Robert Pickett (13) Brighton Hill Community School

PIANO

I feel enclosed,
Trapped like a rabbit, tussling in a snare.
I feel her icy eyes
Piercing down my back.
An old dark dusty place,
Damp crawling up the walls.
The silence is creepy.
One last try at the impossible piece,
Please let me break free.
If I could lie in my delightful bed,
The frustrated waiting could be discarded.
Look at the lucky cat,
Lying in front of the blazing fire,
Not a worry in the world.
The window beckons and beyond,
The lush green carefree world.
Blossoming trees,
A babbling brook,
A world with new life springing from every corner.

Chris Duncan (13) Brighton Hill Community School

THE WONDERFUL NIGHT I'LL NEVER FORGET

The atmosphere comfortable, no-one around.
You could hear a pin drop on the ground.
No-one to interfere or to pry,
Just my book and I.

My parents had departed, I hadn't started.
I began to browse, look, then stare.
No-one would interrupt me, no-one would dare.
It contained everything from victory to terror,
The cover quite dirty, but the book was a pleasure.

I soon began to examine and take it all in,
So peaceful and harmonious, no noise or din.
A book which I read and was totally enthusiastic,
A book which I thought was brilliant, marvellous, fantastic,
A book which anyone would adore,
A book which would leave no-one bored.

It wasn't just the book, the atmosphere was electrifying.
I kept looking around and sighing,
'What a good book, what a peaceful place,
I wish everyone could see the smile on my face.'

I was on my own, the stars gleaming brightly in the sky.
'Oh I feel so comforted,' I began to sigh.
A brilliant book, a wonderful warmth, a fantastic light.
Cry I might, I lay back and thought of the night.

When I opened my eyes, my parents were back,
They complained that I was a slouch and that I was slack.
But it doesn't matter, I can look back at
The wonderful night I'll never forget.

Neil Moir (12) Brighton Hill Community School

8

WALK IN THE PARK

The sun rises over the haze and mist,
The sun ray shines through the dew drops,
Then the birds awake from their slumber,
A stirring seems to appear people playing, working,
Walking.
Wildlife waken squirrels gathering. Birds chirping,
Gardeners sowing, ploughing, harvesting, burning leaves,
The collecting of conkers under the old chestnut tree,
Cooking of chestnuts the sweet, succulent smells,
Leaves are still falling red, orange, yellow, brown,
Then the night draws nigh,
All the children go back from play,
To sit in front of the fireplace,
To warm their fingers and toes,
To drink cocoa,
Then the sun sets in technicolour,
All the children go to bed,
Ready for the morning next,
To play some more.

Timothy Carpenter (12) Brighton Hill Community School

SEASONS

Autumn leaves.
Red orange brown and gold.
Once there were green but now they are old.
Falling gently to the ground.
Trees are now bare above the mound.

Summer holiday.
Great to be away from school.
With my mates I play footbal .
Long lazy days I ride my bike.
Fun and sun this is the season that I like.

Winter snow.
Little white flakes fall from the sky.
On the ground like a carpet they gently lie.
Soon in the sun to melt and go
I love to see the world covered in snow.

Spring alive.
Spring is the time of natural rebirth
Little green buds appear from the earth
Flowers trees for so long asleep
To be full grown a harvest to reap.

Ben Allum (12) Brighton Hill Community School

AUTUMN

On a cold frosty morning
As I walked to school
The gold hazy sun was shining through
The mist
The air was crisp, the colours clear
Yellows, browns and greens.
Silky webs glistened in the early morning
Sun
Crystal drops suspended from a single thread
Delicate but ultra strong.
Jumping in the crunchy leaves
Crackling, crispy, rustling sounds.
I was having fun.
Bare branches swinging in the wind,
Children playing silly things
Happy smiling faces all around
Autumn is here.

Carole Ranson (12) Brighton Hill Community School

LONELY

She's there,
Thinking of what's past,
Sat in her armchair,
With her dolls and her necklace and her mug of tea,
Thinking of what could have been.
It's cold outside,
And quite warm within.
She's upset about someone or something.
Alone with no-one to love or care.

Sean Palmer (12) Brighton Hill Community School

11

LOVE LETTER TO JULIET

To my love from my heart so deep;
My feeling for thou burns on still.
There is no reason for thou to weep,
Together we shall climb this hill.
The friendship we've built shall never halt;
The war we face is upon us here.
Our love is stronger than the sword of Tybalt.
We are always met by anger and fear.
We are strong enough to break the spell
And the families will be together;
All friends and all are well.
Still our love will go on forever.
　　　　Montague and Capulets be one;
　　　　Or soon after there will be none.

Joe Bury (15) Brighton Hill Community School

GIRL AT THE PIANO

She's trapped, trapped in a world of silence,
Yet she plays to her heart's content.
The room is dull, yet outside is bright.
Three chairs and only one person.
She's only a maid and has an exquisite piano.
A cat sits unstartled on a cushion
Yet the piano is loud.

Oliver Pitsch (12) Brighton Hill Community School

FOR HER LOVED ONE, HE WAS LEAVING

She waited for her lover, at the cottage door,
Her deep-blue eyes they wandered across the purple moor,
A small tear filled with sorrow splashed the dirty floor,
For her loved one, he was leaving.

As he rode across to meet her, a dagger hit her heart,
For she loved him so deeply, and didn't want him to depart,
She knew that he'd be careful, she knew that he'd be smart,
But her loved one, he was leaving.

He draped his arms around her, and drew her body near,
'Forget-me-not', she whispered, in his caring ear,
He told her not to worry, he said 'I'm always here',
But her loved one, he was leaving.

He kissed her for the last time, then sadly turned away,
And he rode into the sunset, to join the royal affray,
She watched him disappear, her life felt dull and grey,
For her loved one, he had left.

The days turned into weeks and the weeks turned into years,
Every minute of her life, was shrouded by her tears,
And then the dreadful letter came, that proved all her fears,
For her loved one, he had gone . . .

Claire Furneaux (13) Brighton Hill Community School

THE MURDER

My mother told me never,
There was certainly no way.
But suddenly it happened
My father went away.

I heard him on a phonecall,
They said that he would pay.
I went to school and then came back,
My father was away.

My dad was very deep in debts,
Just why he wouldn't say.
Some men went up into my house,
And took my dad away.

I quickly ran into the house,
I thought he was okay.
I found him lying on the floor,
My dad had gone away.

I quickly told the police to come,
But heard my mother say,
'Twas me who did the murder,'
They took my mum away.

Jamie Lamport (14) Brighton Hill Community School

SEPARATION

Things were going well I thought,
Up until that night
Then the news was told to me,
Things would never be right.

My mum to my dad said 'leave',
I love you no more,
It's not fair on the children,
If you hit them once more.

I can't bare the pain no more
I feel it's all my fault
If I hadn't have told my mum
My dad wouldn't have been caught.

He's now turned against my mum
He's hitting her as well,
Why does he do this?
Can't he see he's making our lives hell?

Endless nights of crying
Cold and lonely days
My life has fallen to pieces
In so many ways.

Have I done something wrong?
Why did this happen to me?
My life has been turned upside down
But oh! So suddenly.

How can everything change so quick?
So much love forgotten,
My mum says he's different now,
Turned from bad to rotten.

Wendy Smith (13) Brighton Hill Community School

TOO LATE

I can't help but start to cry,
When I think and wonder why.
Why there's such a thing as famine,
It's much worse than death by hanging.

I see him sadly standing there,
His tiny body almost bare
What has he done to deserve this fate
It's been handed to him on a plate.

His bony body, hardly anything there,
All he does is stand and stare.
Large and round his swollen belly,
Just like the pictures on the telly.

Give him life, let him live,
No-one should have to die like this.
I see his parents side-by-side,
Gently they start to close their eyes.

'Help them please', he begs of me,
But it's too late, why can't he see.
He's crying now, large pools of tears,
This is one of his worse fears.

Dying bodies all around,
The boy sinks gently to the ground.
Then I start to wonder why,
Oh why did the poor boy have to die?

Michelle Bird (14) Brighton Hill Community School

THE ENDING OF THE WORLD

When will the world end?
It's plain to see why,
It's probably only on lend,
And then soon to die.

As the night drifts away,
And the morning light shows,
The dawning of another day,
For how long no-one knows.

As I view the world today,
I don't seem to understand,
How its life has withered away,
This once precious and beautiful land.

People try to ignore the world's pain.
They say earth will last forever.
But there's all this pollution and acid rain,
The changing of space and the weather.

Some people try to save the world,
How serious is their plight!
They know how much the world is worth,
And won't give up the fight!

Emma Gash (14) Brighton Hill Community School

CHAOS OF THIS TIME

Chaos of this time,
Tanks on the streets.
Killing of the armies,
Murderous psychopathic freaks.
Raging crowds roar,
Breaking the nation's law.
A race against time,
To halt the crazy crime.
Governments' officials,
Speak to the world.
Stealing the trust,
A lie in every world.
War for territory,
Fighting for your God given land.
Carnage, slaughter for justice,
Justice has dissolved, justice is dead.
Rape, murder, disease, destruction,
The list goes on will it end.
Senseless, violent, vandals,
Terrify the public community.
Knowledge is the weapon,
Against the transgression of the Earth.
Find the explanation,
Cure the evil virus.
Sweeping the population,
As it falls to the dark one.
Chaos of this time.

Adam Purser (13) Brighton Hill Community School

THAT WAS THE YEAR!

They walked onto the hallowed turf,
The greatest team that touched the earth.
They won it all and
Done the double,
Took on Europe without any trouble.
The home of this team is White Hart Lane,
Soon to be famous once again.
Led by Blanchflower
Then Mackigh
Whom kept the white flag flying high.
The crowd all roared,
And sang as one.
Soon after the match begun
The faithful rose,
The noise got louder, Spurs begun to take the power,
The Lily Whites,
As they're known
Played like kings on their thrones.
The silky skills
The Greavsie double
Arsenal really were in trouble.
The ref raised his whistle,
To the roars of the crowd
He blew it hard echoed throughout the stadium
The match was won!
Bill Nicolson jumped from his seat
Celebrated with the team who jumped about
Everyone around was on their feet.
The season had ended with a lot of fun,
That was the year of 61.

James Satwick (12) Brighton Hill Community School

OLD MAN

As I watch him shuffling down the road,
I feel so sad to think,
That life has caught him up,
And as time travels on, the end is brought nearer.
I wonder, will I ever be as old as he?

If you walk closely you can usually hear
The tap of a walking stick
In time with each weary step of life,
Through time and age,
I wonder, will I ever be as old as he?

His back so bent with the weight of many years,
And a face so grey and wrinkled,
A beard of silk or satin, he wears
Long and wispy, like smoke in a breeze.
I wonder, will I ever be as old as he?

Lines of sadness cross his face
The happiness long forgotten
Yet in these brown eyes
Lies knowledge of a thousand years.
I wonder, will I ever be as old as he?

Loneliness surrounds him as he wanders by,
His life, long ago out-lived,
On his face shows the tale of 85 years,
All the happiness, sadness, smiles and tears,
And so through it all I wonder,
Will I ever be as old as he?

Jenny Whittlesea (12) Brighton Hill Community School

WORLD WAR II

This is the man who started a war,
and gave the orders
for a thousand guns to fire
and thousands of people to die.

This is a swastika, a symbol of fear,
a symbol of fright,
a symbol of death for many Jews,
a symbol of an evil organisation.

This is a revolver, a bringer of pain,
a hater of peace and harmony.
It lives off anger and frustration.
It feeds on competition and greed.

This is a spitfire, an item of speed,
of confusion,
and many a young man's last dying sight.

This is a funeral, a funeral of hundreds,
all of whom are dead,
but where their final resting place is,
no-one knows.

This is a party, a show of joy, a display of winning,
a parade of more dead bodies of the enemy.
Is this victory?
Is this real joy?
Have we really won?

This is the end of the war, good triumphs over evil,
Or is it evil over good?
No-one has won, but everyone has lost,
Lost their lives or good memories to the war.

WE WON THE WAR?

Robin Buckley (12) Brighton Hill Community School

21

VICTIM OF COWARDICE

I waited, trembling, by the toilet's cold wall;
Frightened; alone; not wanting to live at all.
The anticipation grew; the fear commenced.
My mouth: it was dry, my fists: they were clenched.
I had no-one to turn to, nothing to say,
My words had been threatened by Them each day.
I had no identity, it was stripped from me.
I was nervous, on edge- just wanting to be free:
Free from the jeering, the torment and the pain;
I wondered if I'd be happy, ever again.
The soiled smell around me made my stomach turn inside.
'Perhaps They won't come' a voice of hope, within me cried.
I could hear gossiping girls, grouped nearby;
Why wasn't my life normal, like theirs? Why? Why? Why?
Why was I being picked on? What had I ever done?
Wasn't their conscience telling Them, what went on was wrong?

Abusive voices grew louder and louder;
The tranquillity crumbled, into powder.
I looked down at the floor: too scared to move,
The voice in my head was failing to soothe.
They stampeded around me, like natives from afar;
The vision will never leave me - always a mental scar.
They kicked; cursed; shouted; shoved; They cared not what they did.
As I sank to the ground, I covered my tears, and I hid.
The beating continued, 'til I felt it no more;
My entire body ached- even my bones were sore.
Finally, They decided that their dreadful deed was done,
And They rode away on bikes, into the autumn sun.
The Bullies: they had gone, and the torture: it was done.
Until tomorrow.....

Joanna Mason (14) Brighton Hill Community School

LISTEN

I told him not to go out tonight,
But he never listens,
He was heading for trouble,
So I told him,
He still didn't listen,
He was just mucking about,
It was his turn,
He shouldn't have thrown that stone.
I told him never to run into roads,
It's too late now,
He's gone.

Why didn't he listen?

Louise Clarkson (12) Brighton Hill Community School

ANGRY THOUGHTS

At Secondary School,
angry thoughts are like
nightmares, just waiting
to burst out.

My heart is like a tennis
ball, bouncing
against a wall.

I am all confused
inside, all I can see is
red.

I want to be left alone
no-one crowding round
me.

I WANT TO GO HOME!

Laura Williams (11) Brookfield Secondary School

23

DARKNESS

As the darkness crumbles away,
I feel like it's a happy day.
But things deceive me as you see,
Why can't my life be happy.
But these hell holes each person dreads,
So watch it pearls, I could be dead.

Far away the Germans are,
Every bullet's like a dart,
Seeing people dying there,
It turns my life into despair.
As, people run riot,
As I see my chariot,
I walked to it as fast as I could,
I climbed upon and there I stood,
Into the sky that's where I went
To see my loves be happy again.

Ellene Churcher (13) Brookfield Secondary School

THE WRITER OF THIS POEM IS.....

As intelligent as a cat,
As adventurous as a flying mat,
As courageous as a bat,
As clever as inside a magic hat.

As fast as a dog,
As leaping high as a frog,
As clean as the cleanest bog,
As hard as a boxing glove.

As funny as Zig and Zag,
As strong as a boxing bag,
As never being a drag,
As thrilling as a boxing match.

As soft as a cloud
As it makes me proud,
To be a writer of poetry, professionally.

David Eldridge (12) Brookfield Secondary School

SIMILE POEM

The writer of this poem is

As clever as a brain
As ugly as a pig
And probably insane

As slow as snail
As loud as a broken radio
As predictable as a trail
As stubborn as 'NO'

As useless as 'Take That'
As fun as homework
As interesting as maths
As cool as a berk

The writer of this poem
Never is any good
So stop reading this poem
I know I would

Yvette James (12) Brookfield Secondary School

SHINING NIGHT

The sky is red,
Shivering pain.
The pain is death.
Again and again.

The sound of guns
Kills the hearts of men
That have fought so hard.
Again and again.

Pictures, letters
From dear ones
Are left to rot
By the men who loved them dearly.
The men that nearly survived last night.
The men that were shot
Again and again.

Tired, sleepy,
Shining night.
I close my eyes to end the Hell.
The days go on and on.
Again and again.
Again and again.

Leslie Hewlett (13) Brookfield Secondary School

HOCKEY STICKS

I'm on the field with a TK4
Better get ready here comes the ball.
Mercian and TK are the sticks
Better get ready here come the ricks
And then I mash them with a TK6

1st match so better play good
Here comes my shot in the goal
Oh I score
What a mighty roar
And the crowd start singing
Oh no they score

I've swapped my stick to
a Slazenger which is worth £20
Oh no here comes a hound running
on to the pitch
Who let that dog on, the players shout
It's spoiling the game, get it out.

Andrew Clifton (12) City of Portsmouth Boys' School

HALLOWE'EN NIGHT!!

On Hallowe'en night I had a fright
As the three witches rose from the
Dead as my friend knocked on the door
The three witches came out
And said Hocus Pocus Aller Cazam
They turned my friend into a
Piece of ham.

I went up to the door and
Wondered was this a dream or
Were they really green?

The three witches appeared
On the door step and then they
Said Hocus Pocus Aller Cazam!!
I pulled out a mirror and
They turned into a saucepan
So I sold them at a car boot
Sale for twenty pounds or more.

Stuart Hiles (12) City of Portsmouth Boys' School

THE DRAGON

Strong scaly green sometimes is mean.
Long scaly tail which is used to impale.
Long shiny teeth which are used to tear beef
These are my claws, long shiny white they
Hold my food when I take a bite.
Untamed beast without a care in the least.
Fly through the air spreading his wings and the glory
He brings.
Playing around sleeps on the ground.
Magnificent creatures now have special features.

Gary Skipper (12) City of Portsmouth Boys' School

CRAZY PEOPLE

People that are crazy have...
Hairs on their hands
OR
Howls and turn hairy on full moons
OR
Have spikes coming out of their head
OR
Have five legs
OR
Have three eyes
OR
Speak to themselves
OR
Have ten arms
OR
They might be like me
and just out of their head.

Scott Mussen (12) City of Portsmouth Boys' School

WEATHER

The rain comes falling down,
It makes an awful sound.
Some people drown,
It makes my head go round.

I like the feel of white, white snow,
It makes my face glow,
It falls high and low,
But after a while it has to go.

The wind blows hot and cold,
It blows the washing line,
The poem is almost told,
The weather is not kind.

Christopher Green (12) City of Portsmouth Boys' School

DESTRUCTION

Charging through the rain forest,
Charging through the town,
With every step of his mighty feet,
Concrete covers the ground.

With every swoop of his scaly tail,
Tower blocks shoot up like weeds,
With one steely gaze from his hateful eyes,
Rain forests shrink back to seeds.

With every sniff of his repulsive breath,
Evil can sprout out of mates,
The only way to defeat it is,
With kindness and peace, not hate.

Edward Smith (12) City of Portsmouth Boys' School

FISHING

Fishing
Is the best sport ever
To catch a mackerel
Use a feather

I could go fishing
Day and night
Without a drink
Or a bite

I go to competitions
With my friends
It's funny how they always win

When I go to catch a cod
I sometimes forget to take my rod

Ryan Cathrae (12) City of Portsmouth Boys' School

MANCHESTER UNITED

Man United are the best
I've got them tatooed on my chest

Man United are the best
Their kit is red and black
And they always have a good old whack

Man United are the best
I've got them tatooed on my chest
Old Trafford's the place they play
And some people even like Sheffield Wednesday

Cantona, Giggs and Hughes
Always seem to capture news
Ferguson's the man they follow
At the top they hope to wallow

They were once known as Busby's babes
Man United are the best.

They won they won and won
They try their best today to win
But Busby's babes will never
Be second to NONE

Phillip Randall (12) City of Portsmouth Boys' School

MY NAN AIN'T RAMBO

My nan ain't Rambo!
She don't know that!
All she knows is - she's very fat!

All around our cul-de-sac.
And over in the flats
She's known as the terror of the town.
'Cos she has a menacing frown.

No-one likes my nan
Not even our local biddy clan.
She picks up vans
And throws them out!
And gives young boys a great big clout.

But then one day she turned some heads
By putting two crooks in hospital beds.
They tried to steal my nan's bag
And they called her a really old hag.
And so with that she summoned up all her fat
And jumped up high and squashed them
Flat!!

Now my nan's a hero
The best, the number one
And some boy had her picture
Tattooed on his
BUM!

Darren Welch (12) City of Portsmouth Boys' School

SCHOOL

Why do we have to go to school
Every single day
Listening to boring teachers
Telling us to sit be quiet and don't play
Who wants to learn about history
Learning about the past

I'd rather play my nintendo
'Cause it's interesting, colourful and fast
Who needs to know about geography
Have to sit and draw a map
I'd rather be in the front of the TV
With a tray of food on my lap
Who could be interested in maths
I can add up and take away
I don't need to know the rest of it
I'd stay at home if I had my way
Why do grown ups always say
I wish I was back at school
They can have my place if they want
And I'll stay at home, that's cool.

Luke Cronin (12) City of Portsmouth Boys' School

VROOM

Vroom goes my mate speedy
Vroom goes my mate
He never slows down,
And he's never late.
He's always running about
Which I really hate.
If he don't stop running about,
He won't be my mate.

Vroom goes my ex-mate speedy,
Vroom goes my ex-mate.
Well he didn't stop did he?

Richard Poole (12) City of Portsmouth Boys' School

THE BATTLE IN MY HEAD

Running constantly,
Always trying to hide, to get away
Looking here, looking there
Never finding an even peace of mind.
But running from what?
My own fears,
My own mind.
The confusion I can sense,
But can't figure out.
I'm not understanding my own mind,
And it starts to become scary.
The thought of unpredictability is a good one,
But when it reaches the point
That even you don't know what you're going to do next,
Life becomes worrying.

Matthew Burrows (16) Cove School

THE PIANO

The day I laid my fingers down,
On eight white strips of ivory bone,
Turned out to be the day I found,
The special place within my home.

My friends all died and went away,
And things of great importance waned,
As I neglected everything,
A few close friends beheld my change.

I wasted time before that point,
Fools, in my eyes, became my aim,
When all that I could ever want,
Was inside me and in my playing.

I almost fall into myself,
On days, when acts were forced on me,
My hand and mind will fill no shelf,
With willingness nor happily.

Matthew Lippiatt (13) Cove School

LOVE

Love is kind,
if you put it in your mind,
love can be cruel,
it can drive you up the wall,
out of us all,
it could make you a fool,
you can hire a hall,
for a wedding or a ball,
or you can buy your loved-ones flowers,
which will make them happy for a few hours,
give your loved-ones your heart,
once you've been hit with the cupid dart.

Crystal Hawkhead (11) Crestwood Community School

A CHILLY DAY

It was a chilly day
In the town
Because autumn was hiding round
The corner of summer
Leaves were falling
In many different colours
Bronze, gold and crimson
It were as if a painter
Dropped their pallette
On the ground
And colours got printed on the ground
And had not been cleaned up
I woke up the next morning.
I ran outside
Picked up a leaf and gazed at it
I saw a crimson blush
And a deep purple flush
I wondered how it was done
Yet I still don't know.

Bryan Light (14) Crestwood Community School

THE CLAW OF LIFE

A boy awoke one day from his bed
And out from the floor came a hairy head
First he screeched then he screamed
The head was coming then the knees
It was far too scary for the boy's belly
He brought up food and something smelly
The boy didn't like what he saw
The thing showed the boy a shiny Golden Claw
And said you have to take this for
The day this Claw will be worth much more
The boy asked but what do I keep it in
The thing showed the boy a shiny silver tin
The thing said guard it with your life
If you don't I shall kill you with this bloodthirsty knife
The boy asked, but *when*, but *who*, but *where*
The thing said I'll see you there
The thing disappeared from the very strange spot
The boy felt as though he had just been shot
Many years flew by
Until the old boy had to die
Many said he died in vain
He had nothing to show and nothing to gain
As his spirit arose the thing appeared
And said his life might just be spared
All he had to do was return the Claw
Then he could live his life once more
The spirit did as he was asked
The thing was amazed and laughed
It spoke again this time to say
You have done well and so you may stay
Return to Earth be born again
But this time my faith will guide you along.

Ben Goble (13) Crestwood Community School

THE OUTSIDERS

They don't know what it's like,
To wake in the night,
In a cold sweat.
To think: If I'm ill, I won't have to go.
To think: If I sound confident, they'll give up.
Because if you haven't been there, you don't know.

Part of the problem is that one day
You might start to believe what they say,
Throw your hands in the air
As if to give up,
Confess that yes I am... because...
Other people try to understand but can't.
Only someone who's felt the fear
Can lend a shoulder to cry on,
An ear to listen to.

One day, I'll find someone.
When that day comes
Years of pain will flow again,
To smother the scars that always remain,
But no matter what people do or say,
Nothing can make those haunting memories
Ever go away.

Katie Wilson (14) Crestwood Community School

CHANGES

She stood there,
her clothes in tatters,
her hair's long forgotten colour
was matted in a painful style.
The harsh wind whipped round
her swollen face,
much wiser than her seven years,
loathed, forgotten, unloved, alone.

He tried not to notice the little girl,
how her eyes told of the pain.
The unwanted little girl tore at his heart.
He cried out to help her,
he watched her everyday.

One day she wasn't there,
he wanted to cry out, to cry,
tears welled in his eyes.
Walking past the orphanage he saw her again
his wife would love her,
he needed to try and heal her pain
he was drawn to the orphanage.

She stood there,
her long golden hair shimmering in the light.
The warm morning sun,
glowing on her rosy cheeks
an easy smile on her face.
Wanted, loved, needed,
her family.

Sarah Flitney (14) Crestwood Community School

MEMORIES FOREVER

I'm not just hurting outside
it's mostly inside too
but the pain's not throbbing badly
it's the words that stick like glue.

The shouting, screaming, staring
the whispers everywhere
and the hurt that's deep inside
it's them they just don't care.

But it's the scars that stay forever
and the memories in my heart
like a sharp arrow hitting the bullseye
and the hauntings, piercing dart.

Will these people ever stop
will my hurting ever go
these people must have problems
but I don't want to know.

Clair Firmager (14) Crestwood Community School

A FEW KIND WORDS

The pain that's caused by a few harsh words.
The unimaginable ache,
The fear that's caused by a few harsh words.
The terror and the angst,
The hope that's caused by a few kind words,
The overwhelming relief,
The courage caused by a few kind words,
The terror disappears,
A special person says a few kind words,
And everything is changed.

Emma Clark (14) Crestwood Community School

41

BULLYING

All alone in the playground, a young boy stood.
All alone feeling low and misunderstood,
Every few seconds he threw nervous glances
At the boy in the window who threatened his chances.

The boy in the window who looked like death,
His face so pale, his hair a mess.
He was the one who made him cry,
Who harassed and hit him, he didn't know why.

It seemed 'Death' got his kicks from it,
Frightening the boy into having fits,
Thumps and punches, words and stones,
That tortured his mind and broke his bones.

'Death' was watching him now,
Waiting for one false move, until he fell
Into the talons and becoming his prey,
But he guessed it was life, it was just life's way.

Perhaps it was because he was only 4ft 10
And not at all large for a young boy of ten,
But perhaps it was because he was a rich man's son,
And in a world of poverty, he was the only one.

Alone once again in a world of confusion.
His friends, a happy life, was all an illusion.
Reality is nothing, no-one cares.
He is alone, miserable, helpless and scared.

Stephanie Murray (15) Crestwood Community School

ACROSS THE CLASSROOM

Across the classroom
With her icy stare,
Eyes that are saying
'Look if you dare.'

Lips in a tight line
As straight as a wall.
When teachers walk past
She smiles at them all.

She is so two-faced,
Like the sides of a coin.
Completely different,
But two parts that join.

When the teachers leave,
The line is back.
Eyes like knives;
Prepare for the attack.

I won't let her get me,
I turn my back instead.
I'm not going to be her victim,
I don't want the fear or the dread.

Helen Wooldridge (15) Crestwood Community School

MEMORIES

Memories of past wars bring with them sadness,
Sadness that comes from remembering those who died.

A man fighting for freedom,
Knowing he must succeed against impossible odds.
Whether he will see his family again is a question yet to be answered.

He tries to forget his troubles, he laughs death in the face,
But if he faced the facts he would know that death will soon overcome
him.

As death catches up with him he realises he can fight no more.
With one last breath of smoke-filled air, he passes away to rest forever.

No cross marks where he lies, sleeping, unable to wake.
He had faced his fears alone, now he will rest for eternity.

His chair at the dinner table sits there, cold and waiting for him to return.
His wife and child sit silently, begging for his safety.

His family don't know where he is, nor even if he is alive,
Yet, as they sit there praying, they refuse to believe he is dead.

He died so that his family could have a decent life.
He died for you.

He suffered for you,
He lost everything for you,
He went through hell for you,
And when the time came, he fell down and died for you.

Just remember that HE died for YOU.

Steven Hodge (13) Crestwood Community School

LOVE, IS IT LIKE...

Is it like a thunder storm;
heavy winds, driving rain, pitch black sky?

Is it like a soaring bird;
gliding round the thermals, way up high?

Is it like an exploring moth;
dull, boring, searching out the light?

The thunder storm breaks to blue skies,
The soaring bird returns to its nest,
The exploring moth becomes a victim of its curiosity.

Love, is like the world,
It keeps us in a never-ending spin.

Sarah Holt (15) Crestwood Community School

AUTUMN

Autumn says goodbye to spring
And welcomes the changes that autumn brings.

The trees change quickly along with the leaves
Crimson, amber, russet and gold
The carpet of leaves lie peacefully on the ground
While the trees are cold, bare and lonely.

In the trees you hear the wind call
The fox, red as the leaves weaves around the trees,
While the birds migrate to far off lands.
Autumn copes with all the problem nature gives.

Rachel Rogers (14) Crestwood Community School

REVENGE

I wanted revenge on those bullies,
I wanted to set them straight.
So I put on a determined face,
And went to stand at the gate.

The first came out just before the bell,
He saw me there and grinned.
Then the rest began to surround me,
My courage disappeared with the wind.

'S-Sorry,' I stammered, my throat was dry,
I struggled to make the words clear.
'M-my mistake, I'll be going now'
My hand raised to disguise a tear.

The bullies began to advance now,
Eyes glinting in the sun.
Spitting, sneering, never hearing,
Their idea of fun.

I saw the bullies for what they were,
As I looked them in the eye.
Getting their kicks from other's pain,
Delightedly watching them cry.

If I tried for revenge, I'd only be
Cowardly and weak.
So I cleared my throat,
And very slowly, I began to speak.

'Please let me through,' I calmly said,
And I knew I'd made them see.
To stand up to them. I had to be hard,
Harder than they'd EVER be.

Claire Bussey (15) Crestwood Community School

THAT OLD MAN

As you walk down that road,
you suddenly get a scare,
that old man, still lying there,
quiet and without a care.

You pretend not to notice him,
though he's been there many years,
all his confidence wiped out,
and replaced by many fears.

The dust that he lies on,
the same colour as his face,
he's got no home, no family,
nowhere to go, not one single place.

You walk on by, past his shaking hand
with your head held very high,
he's asking you for a little change,
you don't care and he doesn't know why.

Caroline Babey (15) Crestwood Community School

LIGHT

Through their wondering eyes I see,
A light shining like no other,
Glistening through their lonely hearts,
A sound you hear that cries.

Listen hard to the voice you hear,
Calling from a distance,
Look in their eyes a light you'll see,
Glistening through their lonely hearts.

Melissa Annalls (15) Crestwood Community School

EMPTY SOULS

The first step into the coldness,
The smell of the fresh air,
I hold my coat tight,
And walk into the night.

The clear skies above me,
And the stars shining bright,
Remind of the empty souls that once lived,
But now have given up the fight.

Everynight there is one star,
Big and bright,
That's my grandad's soul,
Where my heart leaves a big hole.

As I walk around the bare streets,
Thoughts pass through my head,
I dreamt about the time,
When my grandad was not dead.

Lisa Robins (15) Crestwood Community School

THE CIRCUS

There it is, high in the sky,
with red and white stripes and flags flying high.
The big top is there, on top of the hill,
in my mind I can see it still.

I remember we went in through the door,
we looked all around, and before us we saw,
a huge stage with lighting and sound,
awaiting the dancers, the animals and clowns.

There was a drumroll, and a big crash,
the ring master came forward and the lights flashed.
'Welcome to the circus, to everyone here,
next are the animals - give them a big cheer.'

On came the horses and riders too,
holding ribbons of red, white and blue.
Then there were dogs jumping through hoops,
they did the course and danced in a group.

Last were the clowns with their bright red faces,
they wore baggy trousers held up with braces.
They made us laugh by getting wet,
they slipped and slopped all over the set.

At last the show came to the Grand Parade,
everything we had seen came on again.
Then I went home I'm happy to say,
what a lovely time I'd had that day.

Jemma Gurney (12) Crestwood Community School

AUTUMN

Autumn is coming
Summer is leaving.
Leaves change colour
Russet, brown and red.
Everything fresh but cold.
Squirrels dart in between
Trees like a powerful arrow
Being shot through a heart.
Trees lose their decaying leaves
Like an old man's hair
Dropping from his head.
Children are wrapped up
In bundles of clothes.
They look like presents with
A thousand layers.
Winter is coming,
Autumn is leaving.

Anna Perry (13) Crestwood Community School

AUTUMN RETURNS

Days turn short, Nights are long.
Life slow and ready, for the snow sheet to arrive.

The round, golden huge like bird,
quietly flying south through the dissension.

The rainbow town a coverlet of patchwork,
hills of copper, roofs of violet and ruby
streets lined for the great Queen's annual visit.

Trees have thrown their clothes on the floor.
A few leaves light up the bare bracken.

Summer has gone never to return it seems.

Emily Ball (13) Crestwood Community School

AUTUMN RETURNS ONCE AGAIN

One by one falling,
Gleaming gold leaves,
Dressed like proud,
Strong dying knights,
Bungying, lavishly,
To the white ground,
An abundance of lineless,
Runaway kites.

The sun slowly creeps,
From behind the chapel,
Filling this sleepy,
World with light,
The wind slowly whispers,
Through the cold meadows.
The clouds all fluffy,
Grey and white.

The landscape, a model,
Still and lifeless,
The birds have flocked,
And flown astray,
The flowers, so colourful,
Have abandoned the scene,
But all will return,
Around dazzling sweet May.

Jamie Brewer (14) Crestwood Community School

THE POWER OF LOVE

Love can break your heart,
It can change war to peace
And fighting to talking.

Love can make you weep,
It can change a thunder storm
Into pure sunshine.

Cupid can shoot an arrow,
Straight to your heart or miss;
Love can cause heartache.

It can give you hope,
For the future that lies ahead;
Love creates optimism.

Some people get confused,
About love and its powers,
But love gives us direction.

Sarah Holt (15) Crestwood Community School

THE MYSTERIOUS HOUSE

Lurking in the dismal shadows,
a house stood,
its past?
Vampires? Murders?

Only a glimpse of light shone through,
the velvet black house,
the trees rustled in front of it,
and the silence of murder.

Ghosts and ghouls every night,
lurking in the velvet black shadows,
a scream?
What's happened?

In the dead of night,
white shadows roaming,
firey devil-like figures,
their evil laughs flying through the air.

Bats are seen diving into the blackest hole,
ivy creeping up the house,
almost makes a dark disturbing figure,
mysterious, isn't it?

No-one knows who died in that house,
only the trace of deep red rose blood,
all dried up, dripping from the windows,
murder? Vampires? Suicide...
Who knows?

Jenny Smith (14) Crestwood Community School

THE WORLD BENEATH THE SEA

The world beneath the sea,
Is as amazing as can be,
As the fishes glide through the deep blue Ocean,
A great white shark swims in slow motion,
Then a shiny black dolphin dives out of the sea,
With a humungous splash! Back goes the dolphin
Looking for its tea.

A group of kippers cheerfully swim by,
They can hear the fishermen trying to catch them but
Don't know why.
One gets caught and it is hooked,
And the kipper is hoping he won't get cooked,
The kipper that was caught,
Was for sale then bought,
It was eaten for someone's tea,
So that's one less creature in the deep blue sea.

Kevin Brown (12) Crestwood Community School

WINTER'S DRAWING NEAR

Autumn's coming to a close,
then we won't have to use the hose.
summer's gone,
and spring is going to be a long way away.
So that leaves winter.
It will be cold soon and we'll
have to wrap up warm,
and have lots of hot sweet popcorn.
Scarves, gloves and hats will be
all the rage.
And that special night that comes
Once a year, when Father Christmas
comes here.

Becky Thomas (12) Crestwood Community School

IN OLD TIMES

Ill and cold, he sits all day,
dying of the cold.
The house is full of echoes, he sits,
rises for a cigarette,

looks at the clock, reads
the local football scores, and falls
asleep at Ian Wright, saying 'I've ton it'
A world that threatens war

gets worse. He dreams of his life playing
football for Tonbridge, Crowborough;
Suffering with injuries, losing, winning,
playing, losing the cup, winning the cup,

Cheering with gladness. Sixty years
of winning and losing; the cigarette goes out.
At 11 pm he says goodnight to his dog,
and takes his teeth out, and goes to bed.

Katie Taylor (13) Crestwood Community School

HAVE YOU EVER THOUGHT?

Have you ever thought about who you are?
Have you ever thought about if you've lived before?
Have you ever thought about heaven and hell?
Are we living in a dream? Who can tell?

Have you ever thought, that the person
sitting next to you could be a ghost?
Have you ever thought about the monsters you hate the most?
Have you ever thought about Adam and Eve?
Is the world round? And if we'll ever leave?

Have you ever thought about the birds and the bees?
Have you ever thought about why branches grow on trees?
Have you ever thought if dreams are black or white?
Will we live again? I don't know we might?

Erin Hughes (15) Crestwood Community School

AUTUMN

In autumn the air begins to chill,
It becomes crisp and still.
Leaves from all the trees,
Cascading in the icy breeze.
High in the autumn sky,
Birds fly.
Away from the coming winter,
Which to all creatures will hinder,
The sun lies low,
It does not want to go.
Away from its place,
Without a trace.
The wind gnaws with teeth of glass,
Ripping and tearing anything in its path.

Lisa Caprai (13) Crestwood Community School

56

AUTUMN

Autumn, a rich season,
The year's tycoon,
A season of conkers,
Fireworks and fruitfulness,
White jungles descend,
Upon the window ledge.

Puddles of leaves, lie here and there,
The season's bank notes, already spent,
Swirling in the morning breeze,
The uproar of wind,
Sending papers, leaves and trees,
Flying, and getting caught up in the
Long, lean fingers of the hue brown hand,
Reaching up out of the fertile soil.

Nights come early, mornings,
Come late,
Darkness lasts forever, the street lights,
Reflect upon the beautiful,
Rich ambers, burgandys,
And cascades of newly minted golds,
Can be collected in armfuls.

Mandeep Birring (13) Crestwood Community School

CONKERS

As bats
Hanging on branches
Cling to their perches
Green, turning brown
Ripening
Waiting to fall.

Looking upwards
I spy roosting, spiky balls,
Planning my attack,
My weapon's ready and waiting
Sticks as rockets primed for launching.

Fired they travel upwards towards the enemy,
It misses and down it comes,
Up it goes again,
Knocked off its perch,
It comes down, down, and down,
Victory.

Drop them, stamp them,
Bang them, break them,
Peal off their protection.
To reveal the shiny, brown, grapes.

Stacey Lilly (14) Crestwood Community School

THE FLAT BELOW

In the flat below he sits alone
like a person on a life support machine
the only thing that keeps him alive
is the tv, the telephone and the doorbell.

But that doesn't help when all he
gets is death on the tv, heavy breathing
on the telephone and lots of bills
from the letterbox in the door.

They make fun of him and
call him rude names
sometimes they throw things
at his windows and doors.

Then at night he lies in bed
waiting for his wife and family
to come home from hospital
but they never will.

Edmund John (14) Crestwood Community School

LOVE

When I'm alone, without her around,
I think about her and just stare at the ground.
I miss her so much, I'm going insane.

At night when I'm in my bed,
I remember what she said.
I'm going crazy, I feel so dead.

We sat there together,
We're in love forever,
I miss sitting together.

I won't see her for another year,
Looks like I have to wipe away that tear
I miss her, I just want to see her.

Alexi Channon (15) Crestwood Community School

FREE

It sat there as quiet as a mouse,
        but not as small,
It was as gentle as a giant
        but not as big.
It was caught,
        like a worm on a hook,
But not as soft.
        The gates swung open,
Like a butterfly opening its wings,
        but not as fragile.
It raced towards them,
        like a bolt of lightening,
But not as bright,
        It raced through the gates,
Like a river through a cave,
        It was free.

Lucy Root (14) Crestwood Community School

60

WHAT IS THE RHYME NOW?

'Sticks and stones may break your bones and words will never hurt you'

When I was a child this is a rhyme we were told many a time, and when
people called us nasty names we just ignored them.
But now we are older this does not work anymore, what is the rhyme now?

When I get called names it is not like getting pinched or punched.
It is worse.
It is like getting hit straight through the heart with a bullet.
I try telling my mum but she never listens all she says is remember
'Sticks and stones may break your bones but words will never hurt you.'

When sticks and stones break your bones the wounds heel up very soon
but the words stay with you all the time.
So why, why oh why do people have to be so nasty.
Even if you are a bit different it is not going to harm anybody else,
so *why* do people have to be nasty.

Someone please help I just need to know why?

In the end I have come to realise that;

'Sticks and stones may break your bones but words will always hurt you.'

Sandy Khaira (15) Crestwood Community School

61

SAVE THE WHALES

The whaling boat sets for the sea once again,
with harpoons, fishing nets and thousands of men.
The boat glides through the sea, the whales' massive home,
harpoon at the ready, for slicing through bone.
Down below in the waters the whales can be seen,
the men get the harpoon, a ruthless machine.
The harpoon fires at its harmless target,
tomorrow once again it'll be whale at the market.
The whale rise to the surface with an agonising cry,
it doesn't know why it's been condemned to die.
One thousand men cut it with knives,
with a last feeble groan it says its goodbyes.
In Britain we think the whales are real neat,
in Japan they catch them for blubber and meat.
Very soon whales could be a thing of the past,
their numbers are decreasing fast.
We have however began to think twice,
they're as big as three buses but as harmless as mice.
Please help to fight for the whales' survival,
against the whalers their biggest rival.
If we don't act soon and begin to think,
the whales could very soon be extinct.

Oliver Hine (11) Crestwood Community School

THE NOTE OF DOOM

The thought he was dead just didn't sink in
He was a friend a mate it was so unreal
I kept on thinking what could I have done
What was he thinking of at the time
His parents thought it was an accident, till I got the note
It said I should carry his thoughts in my mind
At first I thought the note was a scam
Till I realised he would have screamed when he jumped
Why didn't he scream?

I was ten years old, confused and upset
My parents said I was really grown up
I asked why?
They said you understand, you believe you can make up your mind, you're
a man!
I turned and ran
If only they knew how I felt inside
I queried what they said, is that all there is to being grown up, to being a
man?
My experience changed my whole life
I said what I felt
I said what I thought
And helped all that I could
But I still don't understand about being a man, to be grown up
Will I ever know?

Zoe Goble (15) Crestwood Community School

ALONE

She stares intently into the distance,
The tears blur her eyes,
Mummy doesn't love her,
And for her newborn baby, alone,
She will cry.

She didn't know what he was doing,
She was only a little child.
It wasn't really her fault, she's
Just another sad victim of assault.

He was just an old pervert,
With an eye for a pretty girl,
She was just young and naive. Ignored
Warnings she didn't believe.

Now she sits, alone, she has nothing,
Her father tries to forget she exists,
Too afraid to admit what went on
Her childhood a fairytale gone wrong.

Lynne Stone (14) Crestwood Community School

WARS HAVE BEEN FOUGHT

Wars have been fought, tears have been cried,
Blood has been shed, and lives have been lost.
Children whose lives have been shattered lie in a
Cold damp room in fear of the soldiers who killed
their parents.
Why you ask do wars happen?
Through selfishness and want for more, through no
fault of those poor children, so why is it taken out upon
them.
The younger generation are suffering through the
conflicts of their elders.
There is no peace, for one side must win and kill the
opposition, but there is nothing left to fight for,
everything has been destroyed, power, wealth,
communities.
So why do they continued for there is no
honour in murder.
They think their khaki gives them the authority to kill,
No-one has the right to kill. But yet they continue to
murder the innocent victims of their pathetic feuds.
They haven't harmed you so why kill them.
War is worthless, wasting and malignant.

Carole Westwood (15) Crestwood Community School

THE WOMAN NEXT DOOR

She is loud, she is creepy,
She's got cobwebs in her hair,
She plays her music up full blast,
She doesn't seem to care.

She is tall, she is thin
She's as sneaky as a snake,
She's got long black scraggy hair,
She looks just like a rake.

She's got a rat, she's got a cat,
Who's always on our lawn,
They go out on a broom stick,
And both return at dawn.

The cat and her are both so bad,
They ate my dog raw!
I'll just pretend she is not there
Who is the woman next door?

Shelley Chalk (14) Crestwood Community School

THE GIFT OF LIFE?

Unborn, unseen,
No voice, has been.
Heart stopped, soul flown,
Brain killed, unknown.
Unloved, confined,
Although designed.
Their death condoned,
Their life was loaned,
Their life is trapped,
Sent back unwrapped.
The Gift Of Life?

Lydia Partington (16) Crofton School

NIGHT TERRORS

Zombies . . . staring straight at you, walking slowly towards you freezing you rigid with fear . . .

Ghosts . . . limp willowy cries echoing out to you. Standing still with the fright in the middle of the night . . .

Vampires . . . as well, so do beware because you could be in for a scare. They choose their victim carefully and when the moment is right and the church clock strikes midnight he . . .

Pounces

Fiery flames orange and glittery gold shoot up around you, what can you do to get away and still be alive the next day when you could be dead . . .

Snakes slippery and spiders spooky climb up from the ground around your feet, you edge backwards into the blackened graveyard, turn and scream . . .

Witches . . . wonderfully wicked skid to a horrifying halt, behind the gravestones of which under you're well aware of the rotting bones . . .

Bats . . . swoop over your head flapping their wings at you . . .

Lightning . . . flashes lighting up the night and the terrors vanish and you're very relieved at the sight . . .

Thunder . . . cracks and shakes the earth beneath where you stand . . .

Snakes, spiders, vampires, zombies and all the awful things have gone, but now the most marvellous fearsome frightening ghoul - it's the mischievous monster Mum, come to wake you up for school . . .

Louise Mitchell (12) Harriet Costello School

THE NIGHT OF TERROR

Swirling and whirling see through and white,
A ghostly figure seen in the night.
Fingers dripping with blood and gore,
Leaving pools on my bedroom floor.
Howling and screaming, feel terrified.
Am I awake or have I just died.
Nearer and nearer, I'm going to scream,
Oh let's just hope this is only a dream,
It's got a grip upon my wrist,
Then it fades away into the mist.

Helen Rodgers (11) Harriet Costello School

SOLAR SYSTEM

Solar system like a smile on your face
Mar's turning in your pace.
Earth your home just like others
Venus god of your mothers.

Sun like a fire ball in the air
Stars like a medallion on a mayor.
Neptune god of water
Pluto god of slaughter.

Jupiter biggest planet of all
Uranus you could have the biggest ever ball.
Saturn god of the food.
Neptune puts you in a good mood,

Space as black as a shadow
Rings like a halo.
Heaven's as pretty as can be
Hell as bad as me.

Mark Butler (12) Harriet Costello School

SCARY SPOOKS

Ghastly, goblins,
Grotty and green,
Sludgy and slimey,
And definitely mean.

Ghouls and ghosts,
Transparent or white,
Never out in the day,
But always at night.

Witches on broomsticks,
Flying so fast,
Through the dark sky,
Over areas vast.

Mummies in bandages,
In a deep sleep,
White and scary,
And have no feet.

All these spooks,
Come to scare us rigid,
But all the time,
They are scared and timid.

Aimi Dicks (12) Harriet Costello School

GHOST POEM

Ghosts; A figure floating in mid-air watching us move here and there sometimes blue, a ghost never knows what to do.

Vampires; A blood-sucking figure making us shiver comes only at night to fight for his rights.

Zombies; Hands out, eyes closed following you wherever you go, making people scream and run.

Poltergeists; Throwing things here and there, killing people everywhere, making you scream and run for cover, and he's even killed his mother.

Monsters; Big ones little ones whatever the size making people scream and run. Monsters green, monsters blue. Everywhere you go they go too.

Dracula; King of vampires, master of blood, watch out he's going to bite. Lives in a castle, right up high where storms rage high in the sky.

Skeletons; Bones and more bones nothing but bones that rattle in the wind, they shake and make you jump in a bin.

Werewolves; When the moon is full and there is a hill nearby, watch out for the howl werewolves nearby.

Beasts; If you walk on a cold night air, be sure you don't go alone, there are beasts lurking in the trees somewhere. Beware of the beasts that give you a scare.

Susan Hall (11) Harriet Costello School

THE VILLAGE CHURCH

The village church looms large and lonely,
The dark grey stone is old and cold.
The heavy door creaks on its hinges
The musty smell offends my nose.

How many people have been here before me?
The flagstones are worn by history's feet.
A small candle flickers in a dark dingy corner
I feel I'm intruding on somebody's sleep.

The churchyard is bursting with villagers past.
Are their spirits still here to watch us and spy?
Do they know that we bring them gifts of flowers,
Do they want us to visit and laugh when we cry?

The gravestones stand like a silent army,
One loyal soldier at every stride
With tireless devotion they guard their charges
Proudly proclaiming the date that they died.

The clock in the tower strikes slowly above me
Pronouncing the present with positive calm.
History is fascinating compelling but spooky,
Everyday life that has been here and gone.

Karen Atchison (11) Harriet Costello School

GHOST POEM !

Ghost . . . Terrifying, terrible, transparent
spirits swaying around soundless houses.

Vampire . . . Murderous men gnawing on necks
then kipping in coffins after disappearing at dawn.

Spiders . . . Creepy crawlies, crawling curiously,
scuttling sideways and then backward rolling into the bath.

Bats . . . Navigate the night, relying on radar;
pouncing on prey from a very high height.

Haunted House . . . Dark, dank, creaking and
crackling, searched by spooks.

Skeletons . . . Skinless and clanking, limbs loose and
lanky, bones big and breaking.

Witch . . . Hard heart, high hat, wide warts, black cat,
booming broomsticks, cruel cackle.

Spectre . . . Spooky spectre shining white with spooky
faces reflecting light like blinding headlamps in the night.

Poltergeist . . . Always in motion, moving the magazines, throwing
the furniture, untidying everything.

Corpse . . . Underground, without a sound, rotting
revoltingly.

Louise Perry (12) Harriet Costello School

GHOSTLY POEMS

Ghost . . . the ghost was a shimmering image, hovering
helplessly in a maze of madness.

Werewolves . . . Howling, with hair on end. It's turning
back now from a dark, dingy world.

Aliens . . . Greeny, grimy, greasy skin. From timeless
spaceless space.

Vampire . . . fangs, flashing, fearless in the moonlight
blood, drip, drip, dripping from his monstery mouth.

Bats . . . flying freely way up high. Squeaking, surprising.

Haunted house . . . scary, spooked by spooks. Black, bleak.

Spider . . . hairy, called Harry. Creepy and crawly.

Dead bodies . . . blood, guts, gore. Decaying, depressing.

Gremlins . . . sometimes cute, sometimes scary, if you see one
just be wary!

Witch . . . Black cats, black bats. Spells in wells.

Helen Boylen (12) Harriet Costello School

EARTH

Everyday homosapiens are destroying it.
A planet which is coming to an end.
Running for help before it's too late.
Tormented so much but can do nothing.
Humans don't know what they're doing.

Daniel Godleman (12) Harriet Costello School

GHOSTS, SPELLS AND GORE

Gruesome, gory, ghosts are white weary and weird.
Dripping with blood.

Poltergeists pick up people's possessions, and throw them
through the air.

Wicked witches and warlocks work wonderful wicked
spells.

Wizzle, waggle into a fraggle.

Wazzle, wizzle, wazzle, poof, burn, burn, burn, into a
frazzle.

Vampires rampage through the night
piercing people with one bite.

RIP or you will die screaming.
Monsters rip you apart,
it looks like you will be leaving.

The Grim Reaper has come,
I think you should run, run into the night,
watch out you might get a fright.

Night time is dark and scary,
when all the ghosts come out to play,
it makes the children frightened and wary,
and makes them all run away.

Run home to bed to be safe and warm,
only to dream of scary things,
perhaps they will disappear at dawn,
Or will they return as gargoyles with wings.

Thomas Vrettos (12) Harriet Costello School

KITTENS IN MITTENS

Kittens in mittens
Kittens in boots,
Kittens in cupboards
Kittens in suits.

Kittens under the table
Kittens under the chairs,
Kitten up the curtains
Kittens down the stairs.

Kittens in the dustbin
Kittens in the fridge,
Kittens in the garden
Kittens on the bridge.

Kittens up your trouser leg
Kittens up your back,
Kittens on your shoulder
Kittens in the sack.

Kittens in your bedroom
All snug and fast asleep,
Heads and claws, whiskers and paws
All tangled in a heap.

Nicola Eden (11) Harriet Costello School

SPOOKY SPINE CHILLERS

Vampires are green mean sucking machines with blood bailing brilliantly
from their teeth.
A Haunted Castle with shadows springing everywhere, you're scared, dared
and silent.
Martin malevolenced Michael making him die.
Zombies are possessed, posing a problem to other people.
Eerie places make strange sensations shiver up your spine.
Murderers move silently sifting slowly, starting stabbing people in their
sleep.
Ghosts are spooky and spine spanking, moving swiftly shiftily through the
night.
Poltergeists move marbles, marvellously making mantraps fall to the
ground and making people step on them.
Black Widows creep, crawl, call, fall, then mate, then eat the male.

Paul Skeoch (11) Harriet Costello School

GHOST POEM

Ghost - a transparent, terrifying and a spirit, also a sad spectre.
Cockroaches - black, beastly bugs, crawling round like little thugs.
Guts - gruesome, gory gross guts,
looking like a load of mushed up nuts
Spider-hairy, horrible hobbling from leg to leg, with his horrible hairy
head.
Vampire - black white and red, with a horrible spooky head.
Beetle- black beastly and rolled up in a ball mostly found in a place
where it is cool
Fire - red hot and racing after you,
almost like you're saying boo!!
Blood - thick and sometimes runny,
some of it runs through my tummy.
Bones - smelly, rotten gruesome bones,
sometimes you can hear them groan.

Sarah Firth (11) Harriet Costello School

THE SOLAR SYSTEM

Sun, the light bulb for the Cosmos.
Mercury, the messenger of the Gods.
Venus, as blue as ice.
Earth, blue and mysterious.
Mars, bringer of war.
Jupiter, planet of planets.
Saturn, supermarket of the sky.
Uranus, the heavens.
Neptune, tap to the stars.
Pluto, the underworld.

Neil Vince (12) Harriet Costello School

SPOOKY POEMS

Witches . . . A woman of evil and all things grey with her tall black hat
and an angry little cat.
A broom of magic she rides through the night
displaying her talent to any prey she might fright.

Spiders . . . An eight legged animal, hairy or not,
showing no fear but showing not a lot.
Colours of danger warning you off.
don't mess with the spider it knows quite a lot.

Centipede . . . As it wiggles under the horror rock. A dark and
wondrous place to be
as the woodlice and ants will agree,
its long body of shiny skin attracts the occasional hungry bird.

Karen Clover (12) Harriet Costello School

DOORS
(FOR MY SISTER LEENA)

I open the door and up I go
Up to another world that no-one knows.
It's all very new
Do I start a new life here I don't know.

It's all very sad to leave family behind
They're all very nice and all very kind.

I want to go back
Let me out
I can't move the door
Oh no I can't get out.

Tina Patel (11) Harriet Costello School

SOUL

I am a soul locked in stone,
I can't get out as I have no flesh or bone,
I rant and rave,
And try to be free of this deadly grave.

But I cannot be free,
Like a bird in a tree,
Or the leaves in the air,
Free to travel anywhere.

I am stuck in a rock,
When time goes tick tock,
All around this tiny area of ground,
That I must sleep here,
With no-one to shed a tear.

Laura Stewart (11) Harriet Costello School

SPINE CHILLING SPOOKS

Ghouls and ghosts,
Pale and white,
Asleep in the day,
But not at night.

Cadaverous goblins,
Slimy and green,
Terribly ugly,
And hate to be seen.

Morbid vampires,
Red or black,
Die in the sunlight,
And won't come back.

Zombies and mummies,
Have no brains,
Slimy and sludgy,
And can't feel pain.

Orcs and skeletons,
Bony and green,
Are always cross,
And hate to be seen.

Horrible witches,
In the air,
Ride on their broomsticks,
Everywhere.

I'm frightened of all these spine chilling spooks,
That keep me awake at night,
They hide in my wardrobe and under the stairs,
And all get together to give me nightmares.

James Dicks (12) Harriet Costello School

SUGAR, SPICE AND ALL THAT VICE

Youthfulness and tenderness of skin
Everybody thinks I'm beautiful
Don't know how to hate
I was friends with anyone
Baby-faced and patronised
And I wish I could be there again

People saying how much I'd grown
Development beyond my years
Being assessed whilst being progressed
In the grip of my mother's apron string
Never considering loneliness
And I wish I could be there again

Attention was something I was spoiled by
Hardship I could never understand
This constant affection from strangers
Seemed perfectly natural
As all they say is positive
And I wish I could be there again

Only child but not alone
Everybody was my parents
Why shouldn't they care?
Aren't I the centre of the universe
With the stars looking in on me
And I wish I could be there again

I reach out for my innocence
But I've yet to be corrupted
Abhorrences of adolescence
Encumbered in friendships of hate
Nostalgia brings forth the play mat
And I wish I could be there again.

Dave Nicholls (16) Havant College

FOOTBALL SUPPORTER

I'm a hooligan football supporter;
Watch me wave my scarf.
I'm a great English fan;
Watch me drink ten cans of lager
And belch as loud as I can.

I'm a hooligan football supporter.
I'm wearing my favourite clothes,
My football hat and scarf.
Let's all get drunk and then
We'll really have a laugh.

I'm a hooligan football supporter.
Hear me swear at the Ref
And shout out disgusting words.
Watch me embarrass all me mates
And chat up all the birds.

I'm a hooligan football supporter.
It's nearly half time,
I did miss some of the start.
I think I'll get a hot dog
And see how loud I can fart.

I'm a hooligan football supporter.
Oi! You watch where you're going -
Ooops, he fell down the steps.
Let's go and beat up that Frenchman
And tell him where to put his crêpes.

I'm a hooligan football supporter.
That's what you think of me, you're wrong!
I don't beat up the opposition's fans.
Well I'll tell you, I've saved more than fifteen lives;
I'm a fully trained ambulance man!

Andrew Brinkman (14) Henry Beaufort School

POVERTY

My eyes dart across the morbid scene;
Cold faces stare back, with their cold eyes,
And I wonder what has caused us to neglect these people,
To treat then as vermin, and to tread on their outstretched hands.

I pass a small boy of three, maybe four years,
Clothed in a plastic bag and sucking a filthy finger.
As I march past, he gazes in awe at my fine leather suitcase,
And it feels like a lead weight, a symbol of my heresy.

I pause, despite my usual need for haste,
So I can focus my attention on the other side of the street,
Where a red-faced man is treading the path at a pace.
As I peer closer, I can detect the look of utter disgust on his face.

He is wearing a penguin suit of silver, and a splendid silken tie,
With polished, prim shoes and a broad, black bowler hat.
An elderly woman holds a cracked cup to him in despair,
But he walks on, not looking down. What makes him so blind?

Looking from shack to shack, box to box, gutter to gutter,
It becomes apparent that there is an overwhelming tide of these creatures,
For at every crumbling wall I pass, or every dark corner I traverse,
Another wretch springs out, acting as a blackening reminder to my soul.

'Where have these people come from?' I ask myself,
Staring at a weary man taking a sip from his dirty bottle.
'Did they choose to be like this, or was it through no fault of their own?'
Then a further question arises in my troubled mind:
'Or did we create them?'

James Rice (14) Henry Beaufort School

GHOSTLY FIGURES

Firey sunset, blazing alight,
Wavy ripples dancing on the wave,
Ghostly men, stand behind,
Depressed, dark, dull,
Lonely and upset
Isolated
Dead to all life
Apart from who's there.

The chilling wind rushes by,
Wispy screams hover in the cold moonlight
A dreamy, strange figure stands up close,
Screaming out for all to hear.

Stephanie Binks (13) Henry Beaufort School

WAITING

Feeling solemn in the cool July breeze,
The dismal mood seemed to whisper distress,
Birdsong whistling in the rustling trees
The neatness of the surroundings is nothing
Like mess!

Ginger hair waving in the wind,
Translucent skin pale and troubled, waiting
Ebony black child, patient trusting, waiting
Curious happy but sad faces eagerly, waiting.

Rustling leaves disturb the silence,
Faint distant sounds, swirl around the trees,
More noise,
The heart beats of those present,
Quieten as they become statues of the atmosphere,
Waiting!

Judith Stephens (13) Henry Beaufort School

PALE FACES

Calm serene still and respectful,
Fragile delicate flowers,
Rich and deeply scented.
Leaves rustling in cool whispering winds,
Translucent faces watching.
Deep expensive contrasting colours,
The faces pale with no expressions.

Mark Holloway (14) Henry Beaufort School

THE WEEPING GIRL

Tumbling down
the water goes
where will it stop
nobody knows

The bridge is tall
hard and still
crossing the valley
where the water falls

The girl is there
creeping away
screaming out loud
what does she say

The two dark figures
like pillars of stone
watching the girl that's all alone

The sky is blood red
night draws near
she stands alone
what does she fear

Matthew Hall (13) Henry Beaufort School

FACES

Contrast between
Warm pale faces
In the whispering wind
The beautiful scent of flowers
Rich clothing
Around quiet deep green rustling leaves
Expressionless faces
Calm eyes
Translucent skin
In a still serene atmosphere.

Julie Dunn (13) Henry Beaufort School

MYSTERY

Rhythmic movements of the violent waves
Crashing against the pier
The sunset red, fiery, danger
Deserted, lost, left.

Loneliness, I felt as I stood on the pier
Shocked, nervous, mysterious I thought
The horizon contrast I saw with fear
Wind, waves, water I heard and nothing else . . .

The past so peculiar
Filling my mind with treacherous thoughts
Distressed, distraught, disorientated
What happened to me ? . . .

Emotional yet angry

I screamed . . .
But nothing - nothing made sense?

Katy Rabjohn (13) Henry Beaufort School

WHISPERS

The dismal mood seems to whisper distress,
Feminine women in the mid-morning light,
Solemn feelings come from deep inside.
Illness and death, illness and death.

The rich warm light comes shining through,
The downcast crowd do not smile,
They disapprove of the happy birds,
They do not care,
They do not care.

Joanna Glanville (13) Henry Beaufort School

THE SILENT MAN

A lonely distressed figure yelling into the night
On the brink of giving up the fight.

Two people walking towards him
Feeling pity and sorrow
Why is he here today, will he be here tomorrow?

Suddenly the figure is falling,
Falling into the night
The colours merged together red,
Blue, orange and white.

As he fell into the dark blue sea,
His life passed away
In sorrow and fear
A shadow passed over him,
A flash of light.

Nothing.

Jason Shiner (13) Henry Beaufort School

WALKING UP THE AISLE OF DEATH

Forced like a slave,
To a marriage of hell,
Dressed in her wedding robes,
And not looking well.
Indecisive bridesmaids
Some smile and some groan
She walks slowly up the Aisle
Where *death's* heard to moan.

Julian Rowe (13) Henry Beaufort School

KILLERS WITH A CAUSE
25 YEARS OF WAR

Two people quite alike in imagery,
No difference is apparent to the eye,
Residing side by side in one city,
Through birth they share the destiny to die.
But destinies are very rarely lived,
And even less where values coincide,
For them to spare another is a gift,
Their cause is just a guise in which to hide.
Facades however can be overlooked,
The one who seeks the truth will find the light,
And see that their devotion is mistook,
They kill in the pretence of doing right.
When innocents fall victim to their wars,
What more are they than killers with a cause.

Natasha Johnson (14) Henry Beaufort School

THE FLOWER

She was brought into the world by a seed,
Dampened earth she did feed,
The sun opened her small pink petals
But rain destroyed as it did settle
Her strong green stem held her head up high
But sooner or later I knew she would die
The wind blew swiftly blowing her green skirt,
As the insects below dug up her dirt
She looked so amazing just like a picture
But fate stopped me as I tried to pick her.

Sophia Mattia (14) Henry Beaufort School

THOUGHTS

Great unhappiness builds inside her
        Covered by her pale, timid face.
Mild breezes passing chills,
        but everything remains still.
The warm, rich, spicy, colours swarm around.
        As the gentle light shines on her
Anxiously her painful heart sobs,
        The heavy daylight falls.

Georgina Hoyland (13) Henry Beaufort School

THE SMALL ISLAND GROUP

The small island group stood timidly still,
Would they ever escape?
As they stand the boat does appear,
Would they ever escape losing their life of fear?
They move behind their leader,
In her green hooded coat,
As they do away goes the boat.
The small island group stand sad again.

Michael Pearlman (13) Henry Beaufort School

THE LADY IN GREEN

The lady in green stood
distracted,
distracted,
distracted by what?
Friends gather around her,
leaves rustle as they draw
closer to the depressed woman.
The dark shades of the
clothes contrast with the
pale peaceful faces.
She stands very calm looking
into space, quiet and cautious
unaware of the sounds
from the background.
Unaware of everything except
herself.
The heavily scented flowers
danced in the July breeze.
The delicate smell wafts
over to the sensitive nose
of the lady in green.

Kerry-Megan Birkett (13) Henry Beaufort School

THE WEEPING GIRL

Tumbling down
The water goes
Never ends
Never slows

The bridge stands tall
Hard and firm
Crossing the valley
Of hard cold stone

The girl stands still
Weeping away
Screaming out loud
Why does she feel this way?

The two dark men
Like pillars of stone
Watching the girl
Hearing her scream

An orange red sky
Night draws near
She stands alone
Showing her fear

The men draw close
She hears them come
She swings around
They take her arms

She twists and turns
Over the edge
The men let go
Down she falls

She joins the water, falling away
Where will she end? Forever to stay

Jonathan Eacott (13) Henry Beaufort School

POISED

Pale translucent faces
Still, poised, expressionless
Rustling of leaves in the whispering wind
Scented, rich, atmosphere
Crowded, silent and serene
Deep warm clothing
Quiet, calm respectful.

Gemma August (13) Henry Beaufort School

FRIDAY NIGHTS

I sit in front of the TV
Thinking,
Of all the other people.
The people who go out.
Where do they go?
A question
Of which I would like to know the answer,
But more so,
Why do they not ask me?
It's simple.
I'm quiet, too quiet.
They don't know I exist.
But I watch them.
They're friends,
I know mine are out there,
Somewhere.
But who are they?
And where?
No answer.

Colette Hooper (14) Henry Beaufort School

GIRLS AND BOYS

Girls and boys come out to play
Although there is no sun today
Dirty clouds have filled the air
These are things the sun can't bear
There won't be supper and you won't get sleep
The acid rain has made us weep
Spoilt the crops and eaten fruit
These are things you kick with a boot
Rivers and lakes have had enough
Everybody is dumping their stuff
Filthy sewage and dirty cans
These have puzzled everyone's plans
This is awful I'm sure you'll agree
But this is what I can see
You help me and I'll help you
And we will see what we can do
If we act now we can clear it up
If you don't you'll sleep in the muck.

Peter Sansom (13) Henry Beaufort School

RUN RABBIT

Run rabbit run rabbit run run run
Here comes clouds of smoke which blot out the sun
Factories getting rid of waste by the tonne
So run rabbit run rabbit run run run.

Run rabbit run rabbit run run run
Run run run run don't be dumb
In a science lab it's no fun
So run rabbit run rabbit run run run.

Ann Smith (12) Henry Beaufort School

TREES ARE BURNING

Trees are burning, trees are burning,
who caused it? Who caused it?
Why? Why? Why? Why?
pour on water, pour on water.

Trees are burning, trees are burning.
Cause pollution, cause pollution,
who cares? Who cares?
save the trees, save the trees.

Trees are burning, trees are burning,
killing animals, killing animals.
Help, Help, Help, Help,
who did this? Who did this?

Lorraine Machen (12) Henry Beaufort School

THE POOR OLD WORLD

The grand old scientist
He had ten thousand rabbits
He marched them into the science lab
And poisoned them with cosmetics.

The grand old lumberjack
He had ten thousand saws
He took them into the rain forest
And chopped down all the trees.

The grand old sewage works
They had ten thousand tons of waste
They didn't know where to dump it
So they polluted the poor old sea.

Alexa Dugmore (12) Henry Beaufort School

SUICIDE

This is the world that God built.

This is the land
That covered the world that God built.

This is the rat
That poisoned the land
That covered the world that God built

This is the smog
That killed the rat
That poisoned the land
That covered the world that God built.

This is the cooling tower
That made the smog
That killed the rat
That poisoned the land
That covered the world that God built.

This is the rat
That made the tower
That made the smog
That killed the rat
That poisoned the land
That killed the world that God built.

Nicholas Hooper (12) Henry Beaufort School

CONSERVATION PARODY

Friends of the Earth went up the hill
to plant some trees for our future
They came down without a frown
for saving a disaster.

Greenpeace went out and gave a shout
a Whale it was for saving
They saved the Whale by peaceful means
which saved a lot of anger.

World Wildlife Fund flew to China
a Giant Panda was for saving
They returned with the info they'd learned
and all the kids were cheering.

The County Council went to the school
to encourage recycling matters
Save your paper bottles and cans
and show others the way forwards.

Katy Grainger-Allen (12) Henry Beaufort School

THE SUN

Like a great big orange waiting to be peeled,
Its juice of warmth oozing out.

Glorious and gay it sits on a throne of darkness,
Guiding the planets on their way
Through the sea of black which descends on them each day.

How gracious is the sun which burns on all day and evening
Till at last it goes to bed and turns out the light.

Rachel Mountifield (11) Henry Beaufort School

WE JUST CAN'T STAND IT

We just can't stand
Not having land
With machines that power
Mechanical towers.

We just can't stand
Not having land
With sewage works
And drains that jerk.

We just can't stand
Not having land
With noisy motorways
And fields of hay.

But we should be able to stand
Not having land
With noisy motorways
And fields of hay
And sewage works
With drains that jerk
And machines that power
Mechanical towers.

We should be able to stand
All of this
And live in complete bliss.

Jenny Burgin (12) Henry Beaufort School

ALONE

Standing there alone,
Frightened scared and timid,
Alone in a blood red sky.
The ghostly pale face
Screaming but no reply
Shutting out the rest of the world.

People just walk past staring in despair.

Rachel Neave (13) Henry Beaufort School

SUICIDE

The sunset burned a hole in the skyline
as the river swirled and foamed over the jagged rocks
of the twisty path.

The sun caught the wood of the bridge,
glinting on the side of
the thin pathway on which they ran.

A piercing scream
burst the oasis of calm,
Shattered the silence which hung over
the red-capped mountain like a blanket.

Flinging herself off the bridge,
her captors gazed down as
the river boiled up and swirled.

The sunset gave a hot glimmer of fiery brightness,
while the river foamed and swirled over the jagged rocks
of the twisty path
Sending her body down on her last journey.

Matthew Flenley (13) Henry Beaufort School

SCHOOL

School, who needs it,
pinging rubbers at the teacher.
School, who likes it,
not me and that's for sure.
School, who goes to it,
I try not to everyday.
Every year it's the same,
        boring, boring, boring.

School, who needs it,
we do to learn.
School, who likes it,
I do it's great fun.
School, who goes to it,
I do my mum says so.
Every year it's the same
        Fun, fun, fun.

Joanne Baillie (11) Kitbridge Middle School

SCHOOL

I hate school
It ain't cool
Dinners ain't nice
They're at a lovely price
I hate school.

Teachers scream and shout
If you run about
You'll get a detention
If you don't pay attention.
I hate school.

Rachel Hine (12) Kitbridge Middle School

SCHOOL

School today
Unfortunately
Wish we could stay at home
Homework in today!
Sometimes I wish
No school today
Boys have taken the football pitch again
Break time now a long queue for the tuck shop
Whistle blows double science now
How boring.
Over at last
Lunch time it's noisy outside
Netball practice on now it's finished.
Double french my best lesson
It's the end of the day
Home time hurray.
Goodbye.

Zara Davis (11) Kitbridge Middle School

MONSTER POEM

It's as big as a big foot,
It's as small as a mouse,
It's as ugly as a gremlin spider,
It's as sweet as a gizmo.

There's a monster in our town,
It's big, fat and round,
It looks to the left,
It looks to the right,
It jumps underground,
And gives a big fright.

Gemma Hayes (11) Kings' School

CALL OF THE WILD

Hear the elephant thundering,
Through the waving trees,
Then it stands there in cool water,
Resting in the breeze.

Hear the lion roaring
With such strength and mightiness,
Then it stands there in the silence,
With all his happiness.

Hear the monkey screeching,
And swing from tree to tree,
Then watch it as it hangs there,
Staring at you and me.

Hear the elephant thundering,
It's the call of the wild,
Hear the lion roaring,
It's the call of the wild,
Hear the monkey screeching,
It's the call of the wild,
But remember
You have to listen carefully for the call of the
Wild!

Joanne Gumbrell (11) Kings' School

THE HORSE RACE

And they're off
Jellybowls in the lead
as they come over
the first jump
Oh! And chocolate cake
has fallen off.
Now as they cross over the
300 m mark Egg on Your Face is in the lead
Now as they go over the second jump
and Tiddly Wink jumps into the lead
with only 200m to go
but here goes Cherry Bun
with 100m to go and
Cherry Bun takes it !!!

Eric Woodward (12) Kings' School

CREEPING

As it crept up to our door
We crept along the floor.
It was quick, it was slick
It was up in half a tick.
Was it here to shed a tear
To the ones that don't like him?
It was gruesome with green eyes.
It didn't smell such a surprise.
It was lean and terribly mean.
It's teeth were dripping with red blood
And his hands were full of disgusting mud.
Oh God, Oh God, don't let me die!
I don't want to end up a gut for garter pie.
Is it really here,
Or are you just making it up?

Stacey Thompson (11) Kings' School

BIG FOOT

It was a cold, dark, dull morning,
I was walking through the woods,
I heard a wailing noise,
I looked back nothing was there,
I walked slowly on,
There it was the wailing sound again,
This time I didn't look back,
I was about half a mile into the woods,
And I knew nobody would be in the woods,
There it is again, that high pitched wailing sound,
I heard a rustling sound I looked behind me,
There was nothing there again,
I could see a clearing in the woods,
I was sweating by this time,
I was stumbling over everything,
I was nearly running,
The wailing sound had stopped now,
And the rustling took over,
I was in the clearing now,
I could see the road ahead,
My breathing was really fast, now,
I was in metres of the road and *bang*!!!
I jumped and looked back . . .
On the ground lay a costume of a big hairy creature,
I laughed and walked on,
And then a hairy hand was put on my neck,
I looked back I took a gulp,
I turned back and screamed *aahhhhhh!!!*

Rachel Waldron (11) Kings' School

MONSTER POEM

The monster is hairy
And it looks very scary
It's very slimy and smelly too
He's not a very good sight
He gives people a bit of a fright.

The monster goes to town
And knocks buildings down
He kills people and sucks their blood
He likes to roll around in mud.

When people see him
Some run away
And some people stay
Some people hide behind bins
Some are sick
And some people faint
But he really is a nice monster !!!

Lisa Collins (12) Kings' School

THE STORM

It began in the evening, as she came she raged and rumbled,
Her cloak cast darkness everywhere, and
She called to all evils there ever were
To encourage her.
Then she began to blow around, shrieking,
Striking trees as she went,
And laughing with joy - a hideous, cackling laugh.
Thunder roared and rumbled.
She snatched sunrays and threw them, and
The people saw forked lightning streaking across the sky.
Trees crashed to the ground, as she
Raged through the night.
Terror was in every household.
Babies cried, children hid under their quilts,
Or sobbed in their parents' laps.
Grandparents knelt down and prayed,
Wondering if it was Judgement Day.
Beds shook with shocked and terrified sobs.
At last the storm grew tired, the people were lucky.
She drifted away as the grey morning light came at sunrise.
Curtains were drawn, and the people gazed
Over the dripping, devastated world.
Could it have gone?

Harriet Jeffery (11) Kings' School

RALLY CAR

A rally car goes zooming by,
splashing up mud into the sky.
It goes down the straight
at a very fast rate,
and gets to the end it's not at all late.

The rally car comes round the bend,
When it's finished it will need a mend.
They get to the next stage,
They're dreaming for an enormous wage.
160 over a bump,
Gives both of the drivers a bit of a thump.

There is a car in front far ahead.
If they make a mistake they'll surely be dead.
They come in first place having fun
Drinking champagne in the sun.

Thomas Coakes (11) Kings' School

THE BIKE SHOP

The bike shop stands on the side of the road
A bike in the window
All on its own.

Inside the shop are lots of bikes
There are team kits as well
The team everyone likes.

Out at the back
The mechanic is there
Fixing a bike in need of repair.

Then the door opens
With a ding a ling ling
A nice surprise
Someone's come in!

They look at the bikes
And ask for advice
Then look at the chain cogs
Gleaming and nice.

Matthew Arney (11) Kings' School

MONSTER'S OUT TO GET YOU!

I'm pretty sure there's a monster,
A monster down our street.
He roars all through the night
And has large heavy feet.
But no-one ever sees him,
It's as if he's never there.
I've never heard anything like it,
He must be very rare.
He trudges through alley ways,
Always in the dark.
Sometimes round the shops,
And sometimes in the park.
He must be very hairy,
For he left some hair behind.
He pushes over dustbins,
For he isn't very kind.
We know he's very dangerous,
We hear he's escaped from a zoo.
For all we know now,
He could be after you.

Denise Davies (11) Kings' School

MONSTERS

Down at the bottom of my garden
Where the big oak tree grows.
I saw a monster, Oh No!
With big red eyes like cherry pies.
I turned away, and walked very fast,
He started to walk towards me.

I kept running faster and faster,
He wouldn't go away.
There were people watching far away.
And then I heard,
Crunch! Crunch!
Oh No! He's eating my lunch.

I went towards him, and said,
'Where do you come from?'
And all he said was,
'I want more food'.
But, I said, 'There is no more to eat,
Please leave me alone I'm dead beat.'

It was getting very dark.
There were dogs howling very loud.
I turned and looked,
There were no more people there any more.
I turned back,
He was gone . . .

Lara Jackson (11) Kings' School

THE POND

Snails, waterboatman, tadpoles, fish and frogs scattering
about in the pond. Why?

Frogs sunbathe on lily pads that are reddy green. Why?

Reeds dancing in the wind. Why?

Yellow iris flowers blushing at the sun. Why?

Nature's beauty in the pond. Now I understand.

Natasha Jolly (10) Lovat Middle School

MASTER OF EVIL

Why did he do it? Why couldn't he see
the family faces, will always need him.
Master of Evil plunged in the knife
Chaos always passes in everyone's life.

Why did he do it? What's left to be said?
Autumn leaves golden and brown lying so dead
The funeral's been done. The memory has left.
Seasons pass, sun, rain and snow.
The thoughts that thrived in his parents' mind,
have been tossed and turned in the holes of time.
As people age they've forgotten his face
Maybe he'll return to this ancient place?

Anthea Atwill (14) Mountbatten School

A DEVON HARBOUR

The fisherman sorted out his snagged nets
Ready for the noon high tide.
Surrounding the boat,
Seagulls swarmed for scraps
Noisily squawking their abuse.
Adults sunbathed on the black, basalt rocks,
While their children crabbed in the pools.
And in the cliff top cafe,
The tourists sipped their coffee.

The warm breeze carried away the morning haze
The harbour glinted and came to life.
The children spun for Bass from the harbour wall and,
Shrieking, the seagulls followed the trawlers out to sea.
The spirited lads swam in the water
Around the mooring lines,
While the tourists chomped on their food in the cliff top cafe.

Simon Evatt (15) Mountbatten School

CHANGE

The historical church stands upon the hill.
Those peaceful trees move with the rhythm of the sea.
The green hill quietly rests,
As the rolling flow of the cool water runs around the city.
Still houses watch as people walk by.
The shady palms protect the crowds gathering along the seafront.

Jillian Mitchell (15) Mountbatten School

THE LADY ON THE BRIDGE

The bridge was old and worn by hundreds of feet passing over,
The bricks had faded to the colour of honey,
Below, rainbow trout were lazing in the warm stream,
Reeds slowly wafted in the gentle breeze.

Her long grey skirts brushed against the walls of the bridge,
Her parasol shielded her eyes as she gazed into the water.
Her hair fell in chestnut ringlets to her bustle,
Her lace gloves, white as snow covered her delicate hands.

Ivy draped itself over the low parapet, like a green waterfall,
Fingers of the willows trembled in the current below.
The woman felt a chill as a cool breeze brushed her face,
Soon twilight crept up on her,
She gathered her thoughts, turned and slowly left the bridge.

Anna Wills (14) Mountbatten School

ALMOST THERE

Long ago, neglected boats floated in a serene harbour.
Dim cranes hung limply over placid waters,
A gantry creaked and rocked under a mottled whirling sky.
A boat proceeded solemnly through the cold, deep, liquid,
Clouds journeyed leisurely above the sedate, yet stolid, scene.

Now bright coloured speed boats mingle through the congested haven,
Gleaming new buildings loom over the choppy waters.
A pier floats steadily under the smoggy sky.
A boat overloading with tourists clatters through the murky fluid.
Clouds are suspended uneasily over the productive yet poisonous picture.

Melanie Purkiss (15) Mountbatten School

DREAMS

At day there is my life,
Where everything's what it seems.
But at night when I'm fast asleep,
I enter the world of my dreams.

In my dreams I have been everywhere,
From here to space to hell.
All sorts of things happen in my mind,
Flying planes, to casting wizardly spells.

The world of dreams is mystical and magic,
It is like another dimension.
It's not a little bit extra,
It's not just an extension.

There's nothing wrong with real life,
Going through every day.
But sometimes when life is too slow,
I like to get away.

Joshua Roulston (14) Mountbatten School

MOODS OF THE SEA

I've seen the sea as a ferocious monster,
Roaring with all its might,
It bangs and thuds with gigantic thunder,
Challenging Canute to a fight.

I've seen the sea as a soothing mother,
Comforting all in her way,
Moving around in dazzling splendour,
The sea's silvery sway.

Catherine Fowler (13) Mountbatten School

WHAT'S THIS WORLD COMING TO!

The darkness falls
the night grows cold,
Silently
the moon shines on a feeding rat
the stars glimmer dimly
A car pulls up
lights, Excitement!
A door opens
and closes shut
the slam disturbs the silence
the peace of night allows you to hear footsteps
faster than sight a man runs across the road.
A lady is walking by,
no knowledge of the hidden man.
The jump! The attack!
The fallen wreckage
the getaway.
A world of broken peace and harmony.

Jody Bright (14) Mountbatten School

A SCHOOLGIRL IN LOVE

She stared at him from across the room,
Her eyes intense,
Burning into his handsome face.

He knew she was looking,
He knew her wide blue eyes were staring his way
He knew.

The girl ignored her frustrated teacher.
She continued to stare at him.
And was not in the least bit discreet.

He didn't care if she was watching,
His hair, his eyes, his tanned brown face.
He didn't care.

She never gave up on him,
But she knew he would never look
He would never notice her beautiful face.

Lorna Hobby (14) Mountbatten School

BIRTH OF A BIRD

In a small cream oval,
A little bump emerges,
Cracks appear,
Like an earthquake,
The shell cracks and falls,
Like the world falling apart,
Shell falls all around,
Like tidal waves breaking out,
The hole widens.
The newly born bird's beak,
Pecks at the hole,
The egg widely opens,
Rolled up in a bundle,
Among the waste of the shell lay,
A little heap of feathers,
Eyes shut tight,
Little claws gripping the shell,
Soon he will be as big as the rest,
To fly proudly in the blue sky.

Nicola Gosney (14) Mountbatten School

THE BRIDGE OVER THE STREAM

The willow tree sways softly in the warm summer breeze,
Above an old green bridge,
The paint is peeling off it revealing the old wood,
Like the wrapping paper being peeled off a parcel,
The river runs freely through the fingers of water weed,
And tickles around the water lilies,
The crystal clear waters sparkle in the sunlight,
Water lilies catch the shadows cast from the bridge,
The water reflects the bridge like a mirror,
In the hall of mirrors in a fairground,
Fishes burst through the film like surface of the water,
As if to catch a breath of air,
Before diving down into the cool shadowy waters,
Under the bridge.

Frances Tuson (14) Mountbatten School

THE HOOVER

Standing to attention
Like a soldier on wheels,
The hoover stands proudly in the hall.
Then, like a sergeant giving a command,
The switch gives it marching orders
Daring specks of dust and dirt
To challenge its gaping mouth.
All in its path succumbs
To the roaring, sucking monster.
And then, with the flick of a switch
It dies, like the sighing of the wind in the trees.
And once more, standing to attention, it is silent.

Helen Parker (12) Mountbatten School

A HAIKU YEAR

Summer
A cloudless blue sky,
Cloaks the hazy atmosphere,
A warm breeze floats by.

Autumn
Trees shed leafy skins,
Like sparks from spinning fireworks,
Colours fizzle out.

Winter
Colour drained landscape,
The wind herds tiny snowflakes,
Silence roams the earth.

Spring
Sound bounces around,
Life bursts from every corner,
The land is re-born.

Sally Nye (13) Mountbatten School

THE RAMPAGE OF THE TENNIS MACHINE

Arthur McKenzie's tennis machine,
Was the greatest machine you've ever seen.
It helped Arthur practise both day and night,
'Til finally the end was in sight.

While Arther went in to have luncheon,
The tennis machine had a malfunction,
It jumped and danced and turned around,
Then leapt 30 feet off the ground.

It shot the tennis balls left and right,
Arther watched one in mid flight.
As it hit the postman on the head,
the poor man promptly fell down dead.

The machine jumped up like a toad,
And then bounced off down the road.
It shot the tennis balls everywhere,
And they went flying through the air.

Down the street the machine bounced through,
Knocking people senseless too,
'Til finally the police were called in,
To put an end to this terrible din.

They wrapped it up in locks and chains,
And picked it up with a crane,
They dumped it down the city drain,
And Arther McKenzie went *insane*!

Frances Gunner (12) Mountbatten School

THE BIKE RACE

I yearn to start and then the lights turn,
My hands on the throttle and my engine burns,
Gripping and thrilling, the wind in my hair,
The speed and excitement is too much to bear.
I rip round the corner and I turned it at speed,
The one thing that matters is taking the lead,
I reach first position and achieve my goal,
But it goes to my head and I lose control,
The bike swerves madly and it looks like I'm out,
A frustrating end to my fabulous bout,
Hitting the wall with my full speed and power,
My coach watches in disgust and then starts to cower,
I lost my race because I lost my head,
I'm really lucky I could have been dead,
Life in the fast lane is just how it seems,
It's hard and it's heavy, it's dirty and mean.

David Strange (14) Mountbatten School

WINTER MORNING

Cold, crisp, clear,
Frosted beauty.
Frozen diamonds of dew sparkle
In the slanting rays of the morning sun.
Pale blue sky, bleached of colour,
Hedgerows decked with old man's beard.
Scarlet berries,
Crystallised patterns,
White world -
Winter.

Mary Partridge (12) Newport C of E Middle School

119

GRANDMA

I remember her dark curled hair with wisps of silver cobwebs,
her small blue eyes and kind face, a lacework of wrinkles.
I admired her old 60's clothes
The long straight skirt and baggy blouse with beautiful bulky brooches,
And her soft sweet voice and rose coloured cheeks.
I remember her distant little home in Essex,
Feelings of her loneliness, happiness and sadness echoing about the house,
Sad and happy memories lingering in each room.
I remember the front room
The walls suffocated in paintings and pictures,
Her row of plant-pots looking through the windows onto the quiet street
below
Emily the manky old cat hogging the only fire in the room.
I remember the old balcony where she would sit in her favourite loyal old
chair.
We would play in the colourful wild garden, picking plums for her famous
luscious pies and chutneys.
And the sounds of the trains whispering, crescendo, shouting, chuffing
along the track nearby.
At night outside the view of the bright lights and dark alleyways,
With the moon as the shining pearl and the dark shell as the sky
I remember our visits, when she would sit me on her knee,
Telling me about when she was young.
I would sit there looking at her wise old hands
Cracked and dry as an African river bed with huge bulging blue river veins
And a tree of lines, each branch reaching out for miles
Those hands that had seen the world, held a million things!
I remember the cancer that led to her death.
I remember the last time we saw her at the edge of her bed
With the hospital flowers and the terrible smell of sick people
I remember the black Limo and the solemn ceremony.
I remember the tears, anger and guilt that followed.
Now she's gone
But loving memories of Grandma will stay in our hearts forever!

Hannah Wintrip (12) Nodehill Middle School

THE FIRE

The fire pounced on its prey,
Raging and fuming,
Aggressive and violent.
He knew he would win.
He felt the power;
Energy filled his strengthened body
And the fight began.

Fire soared over the paper
Trailing a warm glow,
Sparkling with a strange spirit.
He was a destroyer,
A demolition expert,
An invincible virus
That no-one could stop.

The attacker moved on,
Roaring with laughter
At the paper's pathetic cry of pain,
At its feebleness
So powerless, fragile and faint.

But the fire was ravenous,
Famished, starving and hungry.
He had consumed every scrap.
Now they had both come to an end,
A departure.

The remains of their bodies
Lay in a pool of invisible blood,
Decayed and wasted,
Whilst evil looking red worms
Ate the diseased embers.

Sophie Powell (11) Nodehill Middle School

AS IT GOES DOWN

As it goes down
You can hear folks cry,
Save us, save us
We don't want to die.
Cannons break free
And roll around,
It's sinking, it's sinking,
What a terrible sound.
Waves roll in and fill the boat,
The Mary Rose no longer can float.
Silently, silently,
Under the sea,
Brave men entombed,
Soon shall be,
As it goes down . . .

Gareth Davies (11) Oaklands RC School

THE NOISE OF SILENCE

These are the majestic silent things that you hear,
In the first beautiful hours of the dawn.
Spiders snoring softly as the first sunbeams
Of the dawn finger his delicately woven, dew sprinkled web.

These are the majestic silent things that you hear,
In the mysterious, dark depths of the night,
The large, strong trees, whispering to each other.
Foretelling each others fortunes,
Talking to the wide expanse of blackness,
And the immense eternity of space itself.

Beth Palmer (12) Osborne Middle School

THE OAK TREE

Alone and proud the oak tree stands,
An old wise tree in an older land,
With strong, gripping roots clawing the soil,
It watches the farmer at his daily toil,
Row upon row the farmer ploughs,
Whilst in the next field his son herds the cows,
The oak tree smiles and closes his eyes,
The scene is familiar it quietly sighs,
For three hundred years it's stood firm on that hill,
A lot has since happened a lot more will,
It's seen some great battles that Britain has won,
It's watched a parade and a lot more that is fun,
It's outlived some great kings who have reigned many years,
But now that great tree has very many fears,
The oak tree knows he is the last of his race,
But he tries not to think of the axe he'll shortly face,
He's thinking now of the time that he's lived,
His branches are swaying with sorrow,
Because his hill's in the way of a road,
He knows that they're coming tomorrow.

Sarah Winterbottom (11) Osborne Middle School

THE BIRTH OF THE AMERICAN GOLFER

Once upon a clock so they say, an accident did happen at 12 midday.
At the *BBC*'s main broadcasting studio they put the wrong tape in and
The Good Life was to show.
All across the nation *The Good Life* was in view, the people could not stand
it, they could not believe its true.
With nothing else to please them, they had only that to see.
But it turned them into brain dead zombies.
Oh it was so sad to see.
Tourists came from far to see what they could do
When they heard of the disaster that put the country into such a stew.
But as they walked into the room they saw the horrid sight.
Just one look at the vile programme gave them such a fright.
Running, walking, skipping or whatever position they're in -
All eyes were glued to the TV box. Oh, what a dreadful sin.
Fanatics they were, so they even bought clothes to go with the show.
Soon every shop was tartan clear, stocks were running low,
Because the brain dead zombies bought the clothes they thought would
match the show.
American citizens got it worse, they were affected more -
So much that they got the habit of always shouting *Foouurr*
They took to eating massive pies for the people were full of glut,
The drawback of this daft idea is that they had a great big gut.
The name of golf is a game which the English fellows do,
The Americans tried it out to see if they would like it too.
The story that has been told to thee is of how these people came to be.
So listen to me and save your strife
Whatever you do, don't watch *The Good Life*.

Dax Windsor (12) Osborne Middle School

124

THE OLDEST DANCERS

They stand tall, almost still,
Waiting patiently for the sun to finish his journey.
They rustle, whispering to one another,
Anxious for the night ahead.
Ultimately the last golden ray is lost to the darkness.
Their shimmering audience emerges.

The dancers creak to life,
Creeping towards the stage,
Some tall and stately.
Some wizened old men.
All take their places.

The wind starts to sing.
They sway to the music,
Allowing their green and brown robes to swish
rhythmically.
Synchronised steps show a lifetime of dedication.
Their long arms stretch upwards,
Weaving mystic patterns over the moon.

They dance on and on,
Until the sky in its excitement, blushes pink,
Sending a new day.
The wind dies,
The performers scurry to their places.
The sun blooms.
A new dawn and an old spell breaks.
The dancers are trees once again.

Terri Rotchell (12) Rookwood School

THE WHALE

The sun shines through the water,
Reflecting shivering patterns on the ever flat sand,
Fish swim aimlessly through the weed,
Like a small village in the country.
The weeds sway like trees or flowers,
Blowing in the wind.
This is where the whale lives,
The giant of the sea,
But he is so gentle,
He would never hurt a soul.
The whale sings a peaceful song,
A loud, but mournful sound,
For many other whales to hear,
And answer with this melancholy tone.

He glides up to meet the air,
His blow hole shoots out white spray,
Like a Roman candle up into the sky.
As he takes in the surroundings,
Then as all is clear.
He launches upwards,
The leviathan of the sea.
Driving powerfully towards the surface,
Eyes filled with determination,
The surface shatters,
The spray shoots left and right.
He turns and plunges in perfect symmetry of body,
Back to the dark depths of the sea,
Where he stays till eternity's end.

Rachel Hoyes (14) Rookwood School

THE SCHOOL PLAY

Sitting on the bench all nervous,
Waiting for all the parents to come,
Knees shivering,
Teeth chattering,
Cold shivers go up my back.
They all settle down.
My turn first.
I stand up.
I read the first word.
Then all of a sudden my fear had gone,
I lifted my chest and spoke with pride.

Jaimini Mistry (11) Richard Aldworth School

THE DAY BEFORE

I went to bed, hoping, I would fall
straight to sleep
but unfortunately for me
the night would keep
waiting and waiting that's all I could do
knowing my luck
I'd probably get the flu.

I shut my eyes to go to sleep
but again the night would have to keep
wishing and wishing what would I get
maybe if I'm lucky
I will have a pet
it's time to get up it's just gone nine
if I get a car
I don't want a fine
or there will be trouble.

Mark Harris (12) Richard Aldworth School

SCHOOL'S HERE

Walking to the bus stop
I call into the shop
I look at my watch, hey I'd better dash
Quickly I pay the lady with my cash.

Walk into tutor group
Yes, Mr Coop
Take your pencil cases out
Work starts without a doubt.

First lesson is *PE*
Phew! It's not *RE*
I go and get changed
Oh! It's a pain
I've forgot my shorts again.

Next lesson's drama
With miss Palmer
We're doing a play
Called 'What Did You Say?'

Hooray! The bell sounds for break
I need my crisps and my Double Take
I find my friends for a quick chat
And all too soon that's the end of that

Hayley Pfaff (11) Richard Aldworth School

MY HOBBY

When Saturday comes I'm really happy
Hope, hope, hope I'm riding Taffy
With my jodhpurs on and my boots in place
I hope he wants to have a race.

If I give him some Polos, carrots or straw
I know Taffy will love me for ever more.

Tack him up and tighten his girth, that on the side
Taffy and me are off in the field for a ride.

If I give him some Polos, carrots or straw
I know Taffy will love me for ever more.

I go and put Taffy in the field for a quick graze,
I better get his food ready before he gets in a rage.

If I give him some Polos, carrots or straw
I know Taffy will love me for ever more.

Lauren Smith (11) Richard Aldworth School

ANGER

Anger is like a boiling cauldron
Bubbling and steaming away
Inner feelings getting stronger
And someone's got to pay
You may even run away.

Crying out tears of frustration
Shouting, banging, slamming, crashing
Anger getting stronger
Rage getting bigger
Where will it end?

Mark Leather (13) Richard Aldworth School

ALL ANIMALS ARE IMPORTANT

All animals are important to me,
For some creep some crawl,
Some yell some call,
Some howl some fall,
Some neigh some beg,
But it doesn't matter what they do,
They're all important to me.

All animals are important to me,
For names are all the same,
How about Fred or Barry,
Jack or Jill,
Tiger or Tom,
Jerry or Jim,
Sooty or Snowy,
Names are all the same,
They're all important to me.

All animals are important to me,
Some are fast some are slow,
Some are loud some are quiet,
Some are big some are small,
Some like water some like land,
It doesn't matter what they like,
They're all important to me.

Karen M A Macklin (11) Richard Aldworth School

HISTORY

I don't need to know all that,
I wasn't even born.
At first I feel quite tired,
Then I start to yawn.

Yes, OK, so he was king,
What's that to do with me?
It's not like he created earth . . .
    . . . did he?

I don't understand a word you say,
I just look at you and nod.
Can't you make it more interesting,
Everyone is bored.

It's all in the past now,
Let's just forget about it.
Please!

Jodie Pellett (13) Richard Aldworth School

WINTER NIGHTS

Winter nights are very cold,
To go outside,
You must be bold.
The moon looks down at the calm cold night,
When,
What's this?
Out creeps Jack Frost,
Making everything white.
Everything is frozen,
Jack Frost has done well,
So until another time,
He says farewell.

Geraint Perkins (12) Richard Aldworth School

LIVERPOOL!!!

The glory days are here again,
The Liverpool bird, let out of its pen,
From the days of Keegan, McDerrmot and Hughes,
To the time that Liverpool blew a fuse,
They dropped their lowest for a while,
While other fans began to smile,
But now they're back, without a doubt,
Wah hey let's go, their fans, they shout.

Rush, Barnes and Nicol yes,
The old boy you don't need a guess,
Fowler, Redknapp, Phil Charrock,
The young ones under the Liverpool lock,
We won't lose and we don't care,
Liverpool now they've found the flair,
United, yes they've had their chance, but
Liverpool put them all in a trance.

Europe, it's no question, we'll be there,
With Rush and Fowler scoring goals, 'wow', what a pair,
We'll whip 'em all, no problems here,
The only problems that we fear,
Is who will score the greatest goals,
Who'll put the ball between the poles,
So Liverpool, I knew we could,
Yes *LFC* they've come off good.

Adam Hooker (13) Richard Aldworth School

FIREWORKS

The night is near,
I look at the clock,
The time goes by,
It's time,
Time for the night,
To be bright,
I looked out the window,
It was the first one,
First of the *fireworks*,
There goes one,
There goes another,
The sky is filled,
Filled with light,
After a couple of hours,
Everything is quiet,
Fireworks night is over,
Until next year.

Billy Oliphant (13) Richard Aldworth School

CHRISTMAS

Christmas is happy,
Christmas is sad,
Christmas is the time to laugh and be glad.
Put up the decorations,
The fairy on top,
We give out Christmas cards and be happy as a mop.
I could carry on and tell you how I feel,
But that would be telling,
I'll give you a deal.
You give me a tenner and a really nice meal
And I'll tell you how I really feel.

Samantha Collins (12) Richard Aldworth School

THE HORSE

The horse moves gracefully
In a flowing motion
Running wild
Against the wind
Galloping free,
Across the moors
He comes to a fence,
And jumps, flying through the air
This magnificent creature clears the fence
Suddenly, he's trapped,
Locked inside a building,
He kicks and kicks at the door,
It gives way,
He's free again.

Gemma Pugsley (12) Richard Aldworth School

INSIDE MY IDEAL HOME WOULD BE ...

Inside my ideal home would be,
A large, massive, money tree,
All the computers in the world,
A packet of Quavers really curled,
A little spotty puppy dog,
To rest my feet a wooden log,
An everlasting pot of sweets,
And a
Motorised skateboard to zoom through the streets.

David Leake (12) Richard Aldworth School

MY GRANDMA

When I was little my grandma used to say,
'Eat your crusts and your hair will go curly,'
But I wouldn't listen.
'If you walk under a ladder you'll get seven years bad luck,'
But I wouldn't listen.
'If you don't wrap up in winter, you'll get a cold,'
But I wouldn't listen.
Instead I did the exact opposite:
I wouldn't eat my crusts,
I would walk under every ladder there was
And I didn't wrap up warm in winter.
This meant that I never got curly hair,
I kept having bad luck
And I got many colds.
This had to stop!
So I changed.
I ate every crust on a slice of bread,
Until my mum had enough money for me to have a perm;
I stopped walking under ladders,
Until I won £50.00 on the pools;
And I wrapped up warm in winter, so that I wouldn't get a cold.
I had success at last!

Stephanie Waldron (12) Richard Aldworth School

MY BAD DREAM

Floating along in the American sea,
In a rubber dinghy
Just my cousin and me,
Like two swans floating along.
Splashing, laughing and having fun.
Then my cousin got a bit rough
And pushed me overboard with one big shove
It felt like a lion had just pounced on me,
But this time, fell into the sea.
A great big shark must have heard the fun
And came to look what was going on,
He swam along like a speeding train,
Teeth on the ready and eyes all a flame.
He came right up to the flimsy boat
He took a bit bite
I woke up, all alone in the night.

Emma Paddock (12) Richard Aldworth School

FIREWORKS

Fireworks are pretty
Exploding in the air,
Bursting into light
From the middle of nowhere.

But they are also dangerous
Exploding in your face
You could spend the night
In the big smelly place.

So just you,
Remember, remember
The fifth of November.

Lindsay Day (12) Richard Aldworth School

THE HAUNTED STREET

At night, when the streets are empty,
When the crumpled up crisp packets
And yesterdays newspapers that litter the pavement
Are blown around in the wind
And the tiny, distant stars twinkle
In the bleak, desolate sky,
She wanders around the streets,
Calling,
Calling for her son.
She holds her lantern up,
And pulls her cape tightly around her as
The cruel December wind nips
Her pale, translucent skin.
Her wails are
The yearning for the end of an eternity of suffering
The pain and anguish of loneliness.
And when the clock strikes twelve she
Blows out the candle in her lantern
And disappears in the mist.

Callie Wood (12) Richard Aldworth School

THE WEDDING

Friday the 2nd of September
        Was a special day,
For dad and Sue got married
        I was a bridesmaid for them.
I wore a long pink flowing dress
        And Caroline had one too,
But on that day we both agreed
        We really hated them shoes.

Dad he wore a waistcoat
        Jazzy as can be
When he undid his buttons you needed,
        Sunglasses to see.
The pattern it was Jungle Book,
        Baloo, Shere Khan and more,
He had some socks that did so match
        But they were not quite so bright,
He says he's going to wear this suit to work forever more.

Dad and Sue are still married
        And happy as can be
On their honeymoon they went
        To Turkey so they could see
The lovely carpets being made
        And lots of jewellery
Sometimes I think it would of
        Been nice if they had taken me.

They made a vow to stay married
        For life and evermore
I do hope that will happen
        Cause I couldn't cope with anymore.

Samantha Wheldon (12) Richard Aldworth School

LITTLE BROTHER

He won't leave me alone,
He keeps pestering
Winding and winding me up,
All the time,
He won't stop.
Then
Suddenly
I hit,
He cries
He gets revenge
So I pester,
Wind him up
Won't leave him alone,
Now we're even.

Joanna Riley (13) Richard Aldworth School

WAITING

He stands there alone waiting,
Waiting for what?
The wind ruffles his hair
He smoothes his hands,
His baby soft hands,
Over his short blonde hair,
The sun, shining over him
Makes him look older
Older from waiting,
Waiting for what?

Lucy Smith (13) Richard Aldworth School

AUTUMN FUN

In autumn the leaves
Fall down from the trees
All red and all brown
But not green.

They fall from the trees
With the slightest of breeze,
In a big heap all down on the ground.

We jump and we leap all about
We sing, we cry and we shout.
Rolling about in the leaves
That fall down from the trees
It gets so cold we might freeze.

The frost crisps the leaves,
That fall from the trees,
In the season of sniffles and
Sneeze!

Natalie Hills (12) Richard Aldworth School

MY NEXT DOOR NEIGHBOUR'S CAT

She flies through the air
I don't know why she does it,
I suppose it's just to catch a bird,
But most of the time it doesn't work.
If they see a little mouse,
They make a quick sudden jerk and bang!
The mouse is gone,
She takes it behind the bike shed,
And feasts until the mouse is dead,
When dad comes to mow the lawn,
She runs right out of sight,
Goes somewhere so she can't have a fight,
She goes next door to get a fish,
All you hear is a splish
Then a meow, then a cry,
Then she comes and we get her dry,
She tries to get a little bird,
But they were hiding up a tree you see,
She runs past and we shout mush,
She runs into the little bush,
She won't do it again.

Ben Dawe (11) Richard Aldworth School

CAT

Cabaret, Calypso bands
Make me want to dance on sand,
Calories and Cakes
Make my tummy sound like earthquakes.
Cantering around a field
Happy this makes me feel.
But wonderful all these words may be
These words that begin with the letter C
The best word is Cat you see
Because cats can be carefree, no worries, no doubts,
They also can be careful of strange things about,
Cat's the best word that begins with C.
Catamarans jumping over the waves
For this adventure, I have a crave.
Chaffinches, chirp and sing,
This little bird makes me grin,
Cheetahs they are so swift,
For God gave them a special gift.
But wonderful all these words may be,
These words that begin with the letter C
The best word is Cat you see,
Because cats can be carefree, no worries, no doubts,
They also can be careful of strange things about
Cat's the best word that begins with C.

Sally Williams (11) Richard Aldworth School

THE LAST TEASPOON

When I do the washing up
Which isn't very often
I'm halfway through, happy as can be
But when I'm finished
And empty out the bowl
There has to be
A teaspoon at the bottom.
It really bugs me
The way you check and check
But you never can find anything
I call this
The last teaspoon.

Marc Lilly (12) Richard Aldworth School

ALL I WANT IS A PET

All I want is a dog,
Any dog,
A labrador, retriever or poodle.

All I want is a hamster,
Any hamster,
A Russian, Chinese or any kind of one.

All I want is a rabbit,
Any rabbit,
Long eared, lop eared, dwarf.

All I want is a pet,
Any pet,
Dog, hamster, rabbit.
Why can't I have a pet?

Katie Bennett (11) Richard Aldworth School

RABBIT

Rabbits, rabbits big or small.
They are soft and furry and I love them all
They run about their hutch all day,
And when I come home from school I let them out to play.

In the garden they run around
Free and wild they leap and bound.
And when it's time to go to bed
They run up their ramp and bump their heads.

Daniel Bailes (12) Richard Aldworth School

MANCHESTER UNITED AND RYAN GIGGS

Man Utd are the best they can beat all the rest.
Ryan Giggs is our man, I am his number one fan.
I dream about Man Utd in my nest that's why they can beat all the rest.

Ryan Giggs is a superstar he's my man in the stars
Man Utd rest in my nest.
So after that we have a cup of tea, then go home for
Our daily tea (dinner).

Ryan Giggs is so good at football and he is tall.
I can't see him in the mall so I give him a call.
I am a fool because the world is too small to
See Ryan Giggs.

Natasha Sturdy (11) Richard Aldworth School

HORROR

Dracula
The long lost vamp
Frankestein
The monster with cramp
The Hunch Back of Notre Dame
And the beast
With teeth so sharp
Like diamonds bright.

Down they came one dark, dark night
Leaving destruction everywhere they go
Out come the villagers shouting
'Oh no'
As they came to a tavern
They asked for three tankards of ale
And one cup of blood.

No cup of blood the owner would sell
He sent the vampire to drink from the well
But Dracula got mad
And bit the owner which made him sad.

Now they're gone their separate ways
The vampire in Transylvania
Frankenstein returned to the Alps
The Hunch Back went back to his village.

While the beast never found a home
And wandered all over the earth
Searching for the home he would never find.

Richard Smith (11) Richard Aldworth School

RAGES AND PARADISE

Paradise is paradise,
Bright and nice,
The sun is shining,
Sparkling with delight.

Paradise, the moon shining
The palm trees swaying,
While the waves are splashing
The sky is clear as the beach is silent.

Rages of the night,
Rages of the day,
Rages of the clouds, while they flood the city,
Rages of the sea, with the waves roaring with might,
Rages of the storm, with the thunder and lightning strikes,
Rages of the humans, with their mighty blows,
Rages of beasts, roaring with might,
Rages of the worlds, with their volcanic eruptions,
Rages of the worlds, with the earth quakes killing many people.

Ryan Rambaccussing (11) Richard Aldworth School

THE SWAN

There's the swan gliding through the water,
In the light of the shimmering moon.
Let's watch her swimming smoothly,
We won't go home too soon.

She wears her silver crown as princess
Of the lake,
You can have anything you want,
But her you cannot take.

Natalie Stanton (11) Richard Aldworth School

BIRTH OF EVIL

This morning
The sun was born from frost.
A halo glistened mockingly
Imitating God.
Ribbons of iced gold
Flew like kites but
Froze.
Still born in the wind.
Silently you moan,
I am staring too intently
My eyes begin to bleed,
Pitifully
But I don't care.

Poie-Yun Li (16) Richard Huish College

THE STORY TELLER

A shivered husky voice, it complains as it tells the stories.
A way of confusion all those times behind it,
now seems to blow at such force into a sand dune.
So sensitive to the cold, too much so,
the time will run out eventually and he knows it,
that's what makes it so sad you see,
that's what makes being old the biggest task.
So insecure, so alone, so cry it out, it never leaves,
the pain, the misery, who loves you that much to remember
your memories forever.
You seize for a motion, become slow in your quick decisions,
it makes you angry to see them play, so joyful, so happy.
You can't be that again, never.
That's what makes it so sad you see,
the fact that it's growing old, your body, your mind deteriorates,
like yesterdays youth.
Nothing passes by to you but the world flies by alone so free with
every young.
Once a boy of fourteen, now eighty and growing yet more.
It's going on till the end,
that's what makes it so sad you see,
it's going to end your life, it was given to you of such free will,
how can they take it back!
No more sharing, no more relationships.
He'll sit there and shiver till the very end,
then his family will miss the stories he told in his husky voice.

Kelly Spark (15) Ringwood School

AN AUTUMN'S EVENING VIEW

And a cat prowls across the lawn,
And a leaf floats across the sky in mid flight,
And a bush wavers in the wind,
And golden leaves strewn all over the place,
And a bird pecks at the ground,
And a dog howls in the distance,
And smoke billows out from the chimneys,
And lights start turning on,
And mist starts to form in the distance,
And the moon hangs lonely in the sky,
And the washing on the line gets taken
                              down for the night,
And all of these things make for a
peaceful autumn's evening.

David Bellwood (12) Salesian College

MY DOG

Man's best friend they say is dog,
A plan of nature laid down by God.

He calls by the name of Dodger,
And his nickname is Dodger the Rodger.

His famous trick,
Is to be sick.

Over the next door's bunny,
He thinks this is all so funny.

He is a Jack Russell,
And his chest has a multitude of muscles.

He goes wild,
Once in a while.

Man's best friend they have to say is dog.

Simon Reeves (11) Salesian College

HE IS HOLLOW

What's left inside him? Why can't he remember us?
Can't he hear us? We were once brothers.
We talked for hours last week, about what we wanted to be
I sit now with his hand in mine, but I know he can't feel.

No-one knows what's done is done,
      It's as if he were dead.

I'm close with our mother, and she cries endlessly,
Lord how we miss him, at least what's remembered.
It was so important, to have a brother in life,
But it's hard when my brother lies with blank expression.

No-one knows what's done is done,
      It's as if he were dead.

He's as hollow as I, alone now
He's as hollow as I, alone, a shell of a man
Just flesh and bone.

There's no soul, he sees no love,
Mad at God I shake with anger at skies above.

He is hollow as I converse
I wish he'd waken from this curse
To hear my words before its through
My brother I want to follow you.

No-one knows what's done is done, it's as if he were dead,
He's as hollow as I, alone, now,
He's as hollow as I, alone.

Duncan Williams (13) Salesian College

THE DESERTED BEACH

In the glowing of the night
In the pale shade of light,
That is the moon and stars
I walk along the beach,
And see the tongues of water, lap the shore,
And the grass on the cliff, rustle in awe -
At the splendour of the sea and sky
I think, how many have died -
At the brutal fists of all the seas -
How many have lived, to tell its strength?
I hear a howl, a ghostly noise,
I look to the sea and poised . . .
I want to run, I know I won't.
As unicorns, I see afloat,
Charging at me on the waves,
Heads thrust down and
Wearing their horns, like a crown
I shield my eyes from the glare of theirs,
And suddenly the salty air fills my lungs,
And there I stand, like a broken toy
The foam engulfs me, and plasters my hair
I look to the line where sea meets sky
And there a unicorn rears high
With the sun, in the morning sky.

Alexander Grimwood (12) Salesian College

MTV

It goes on in the morning,
as soon as I get up.
I put the cornflakes in their bowl,
And the coffee in a cup.

I tune into MTV
My dad says it's too early and too loud.
I turn over to channel four
I can have breakfast with a crowd.

I get ready for and go to school,
I've had to turn it off.
For six and a half hours I feed my brain
At 3.30 I switch off.

I arrive home at 3.40
I run in and switch on MTV again,
My dad comes in and says homework
Turn it off are you insane?

My homework is completed,
Hooray! I turn on MTV
Oh no! It's time for dinner
There's no MTV for me.

The dinner is all eaten
And the plates are all clean,
I'm heading for the living room but my dad
Is watching the news he's already seen.

My brother practices the piano
It lasts till I go to bed,
My dad says MTV is bad for me
And I should read a book instead.

Robin Carter (11) Salesian College

STEAM TRAINS

The steam train rolls into the station;
It is quickly decreasing in speed.
It comes to a halt and the passengers get on;
Now the train carries on with its deed.

The train's getting faster and faster.
The smoke is now pouring out.
The hooter is sounded and the carriage goes dark
And the children, with glee, start to shout.

The train rushes into the open.
The tunnel is soon far behind.
As it approaches the hill, the train's surrounded by trees
And, amongst them, the tracks need to wind.

The train huffs and puffs up the hillside.
It struggles to get to the top -
The train, with a whoosh, hurtles down to the sea
And then battles to grind to a stop.

Past rivers and fields we have been,
With factories and houses as well.
The smoke coming in has blackened our skin -
Where we've been is easy to tell!

The steam train rolls into the station;
It is quickly decreasing in speed.
It comes to a halt and the passengers leave.
Once more the train's fulfilled its deed.

Jeremy Honeywill (13) Salesian College

THE FAMINE

The poor will be with you always
People die, people cry,
The hot sun is blazing down
There is no food, there is no water
They all sit and dream of slaughter
Why is it us?
Why not them?
Please come and rescue me and my son,
There is no shade,
We are very poor,
And don't you forget,
There is no cure.

Julie Chancellor (14) Sholing Girls' School

THE LONELY STRANGER

Through the hallway I could barely see
A strange white figure staring at me
His shadow slowly moved towards the door
So I turned around and lay on the floor.

I crawled along that hard cold ground
To see that shadow just walk around
It wasn't until it came up to me
I jumped in the air and fell on my knee.

It started walking up the stairs
I then started to think of all these dares
It then grabbed hold of the scruff of my neck
I turned around and it gave me a peck.

Karlene Maunder (14) Sholing Girls' School

ODE

My nan's always counting calories
My mum's always drinking tea
My grandad's always sitting down and
                                    watching the TV
My dad's always watching football
My cousin's always playing games
And then there's me, who is oh but a
Pain but perfect in some way and I
Love all my family too!

Claire Hill (12) Sholing Girls' School

TEACHERS HAVE FEATURES

Teachers have features
Teachers have brains
Old fashion teachers gave you the cane.

Teachers teach English
Teachers teach Maths,
Old fashion teachers made you wear a dunce's hat.

Teachers teach history
Teachers teach games,
Old fashion teachers made you march down the lane.

Teachers have features
Teachers have brains
Old fashion teachers gave you the cane.

Nicola Freeman (11) Sholing Girls' School

ODE ON BABYHOOD

When I was about one or two,
Into a little pain I grew.
I made the cat's life seem hell,
But I really like it now.
I wrecked the lovely family shawl,
It had been in the family for years, I'm cruel.
I drowned my hamster in the sink,
I was only two or three, I think.
So you see I was a pain,
But I'll never be like that again.

Kristin White (13) Sholing Girls' School

AUTUMN

The summer is over
Autumn is here
Let's go out
And have a beer.

Leaves are falling all around
Rusty red and golden brown
Frosty mornings will be here for a while,
I wish I was on a boat up the Nile.

All the wind and all the rain
Running down the window pane
I wish that autumn will not come
Because my ears will go all numb.

Catherine Dickson (14) Sholing Girls' School

DREAMER

Through the window the moon light streams,
A lonely girl sits and dreams.

Her only love has gone away
Maybe he will come back one day.

A pretty face that once did glow
With passionate love of man did know.

Spent in days dreams waiting for
Her love whom she did adore.

Perhaps there will soon come a day
When love will wipe her tears away.

For now she'll spend these lonely years
Smiling through her love torn tears.

Sherene Menage (14) Sholing Girls' School

DILLY, MILLY AND BILLY

There was a young dog called Dilly
Who was such a silly billy
She saw her mate Milly
Who said you look silly.
Then Milly saw the cat Billy
So Milly chased Billy
And Billy chased Milly
So Dilly chased Milly and Billy.

Catherine Passingham (14) Sholing Girls' School

SMOKING

If you smoke
You are a joke
You think you look smart
But you look like a piece of really bad art.

You think you look cool
But you look like a fool
So for your own health you had better
Start thinking
Before you really start stinking.

Your teeth will go yellow
Your mind will too
Don't get me wrong
I am saying this for you.

You spend all your money
And blow it up in smoke
Stop and think you are a joke.

Tracy Smith (14) Sholing Girls' School

SEASONS

Summer, autumn, winter, spring
Seasons all around.
Spring is here and flowers sprout
And buds fall to the ground.
Snow starts falling in the fields
And creatures start to run,
Winter is a happy time
But then out comes the sun.
Autumn comes and trees fall dead
And leaves fall to the ground,
Children playing happily
Kicking them around
Playing in the garden
It is very hot.
Jumping in the paddling pool
Getting wet a lot.

Keri Trueick (11) Sholing Girls' School

THE WIND

I love to hear the wind
Whistling through the trees
When I go to bed
I feel the lovely breeze.

I love to feel the wind
Ruffling in my hair
I cannot ever see it
But I know that it is there.

Maria Tarrant (14) Sholing Girls' School

GRANDAD

When I was five I had a grandad
Grandad Edward was his name
But one awful day on the 8th of June
I knew I'd never see him again.

I used to sit upon his knee
While he would make me laugh
The last I saw of Grandad Ted
Was him walking down the path.

My mother said his heart had stopped
I saw my father cry
I didn't know what was going on
However hard I tried.

I sometimes think of Grandad now
When I stare up at the moon
'Goodnight Grandad Edward
We'll meet again quite soon.'

Gemma Smith (13) Sholing Girls' School

MEW

Mew is my cat
And she's very fat
She's tall and very round.
She loves to eat and fall asleep
In her favourite chair.
She claws me very hard
When I hold her very tight
And when I fall asleep
She's sat right by my feet.

Sharon Watts (14) Sholing Girls' School

SAD

I'm feeling sad when shall I do?
I can't think what to say.
So I'll make it sport, now don't you talk
It's not my lucky day!

Lisa Nicholls (14) Sholing Girls' School

TO BE INSENSITIVE

To look
without seeing.
To hear
without listening.
To sniff
without smelling.
To taste
without savouring.
To touch
without feeling.
To know
without understanding.
To be
without sensitivity.

Miriam Dauvin (14) Sholing Girls' School

LOVE

When I was in love, you see
I thought this love was meant to be
Then one day someone said
'Love is never meant to be.'
Then they sat me down for me to see
That my boyfriend had soon left me
So you see love is not for me . . .
But now you see love is for me
Soon my love will be over because
Love is never meant to be.

Michelle Bunday (14) Sholing Girls' School

MY FAVOURITE FOOD

My favourite food is pizza and chips
And also sausages and mash.
I quite like spaghetti bolognese
But I hate any kind of quiche.

My favourite desert is lemon meringue,
And also strawberries and cream.
Raspberry jelly isn't a favourite of mine
But chocolate ice-cream, a dream.

My favourite drink is cherryade
And also lemon and lime
Lemonade is refreshing and cool
But clear water, for me, is fine.

My favourite sweets are chocolate eclairs
And also Smarties and Twix.
Turkish Delight I don't really like
But I really like cheese sticks.

Sadie Broomfield (11) Sholing Girls' School

LITTLE BIRD

Around the world in eighty days
Across the sea and sky
Could this be how long it takes for little birds to fly
Before they find a nesting place no longer then to roam
But sit and twitter to their friends
There is no place like home.

Karli Benneyworth (12) Sholing Girls' School

MY BIRD

My bird is boring at times
It doesn't sing or talk,
It just walks on its grit,
Laying on the bottom of the cage
Collecting feathers and pips.

The colour of my bird is weird,
The colours are all over the place,
Some are yellow, some blue,
God knows they could be green
Or they could be red you know.

He has got lots of toys
They're all over the top
He does twists on his swing
Or sometimes he just likes looking at himself
He probably thinks he's the best.

But I love him
And he loves me too.
We both know it
Even though we can't talk to each other
I know it because I can see it in his eyes
He probably sees it in mine too.

Alexandra Starr (11) Sholing Girls' School

HUMPHREY THE CAT

There once was a cat named Humphrey
And he wasn't exactly brave.
He was a little scaredy cat,
Unlike his elder brother Dave.
So when the princess of the town,
Was kidnapped and locked in a cave
Humphrey built up all his courage,
And to her, whom he went to save.

Humphrey wanted to go that night,
Although he was scared of the dark,
He wanted to go the long way,
Rather than risk it through the park!
As Humphrey crept towards the cave,
His little paws began to shake.
'Hello' he cried, inside the cave
As his voice began to break!

Humphrey spotted a light ahead,
Even though it was rather dim,
He started to creep towards it,
Though he was shaking limb from limb.
As Humphrey approached the dim light,
His heart beat went back to normal,
There stood before him the princess
Kissing, with the Duke of Cornwall!

But when the princess saw Humphrey
She hugged him and gave him a squeeze,
She then turned to the gob smacked Duke
And shouted, 'Go away, you sleeze!'
They both fell in love straight away,
And the pair were instantly wed
You might think it strange as I do,
But that's how the story is said!

Lauren Hancock (14) & Kirsty Maunder (13) Sholing Girls' School

WHEN THE CHURCH CLOCK STRIKES TWELVE

The clock strikes twelve
The ghosts come out
The witches fly about
The goblins hide behind rubbish bins.

The bats have races
Who will win?
The big giants walk around
Taking children who were sleeping safe and sound.
The clock strikes one
They hide away
No more monsters 'til it's gone another day.

Jessica Tory (11) Sholing Girls' School

CRIES OF PAIN

What goes on in their minds?
To all of this are they totally blind?
The anger, the hate, the suffering, the pain
From all of this, will anyone gain?

Who will benefit from all this fear?
Who will shed the very last tear?
The damaged feelings, will they ever mend?
And all of this, will it ever end?

Maybe one day this will all be gone
The world will be free from all this wrong.
We'll wake up one day it maybe tomorrow,
And the whole world will be happy and free from sorrow.

Will we ever forget those who kill?
Only time will tell, only time will heal.

Lucy Hyde (14) Sholing Girls' School

AUTUMN

Leaves blowing all over the ground,
Making a very crispy sound.
All the trees are looking bare,
As if they don't even care.
People standing on the leaves,
Someone's falling on their knees.
The leaves are yellow, brown and red,
Oh look, one's fallen on his head!

Sara Hills (11) Sholing Girls' School

HOMEWORK

Homework is a bore
It makes me want to snore.
It's not that I don't do it,
But it makes me want to roar.

I used to come home from school
And play a bit of ball,
Watch a bit of TV
And drink something nice and cool.

Now all I do when I come in from school
Is homework,
What a bore.
You'd think from a hard working day at
School,
They'd give you a rest from it all.

I suppose I can't complain
But I don't have fun anymore.
Oh homework is such a bore.

Sophie Denton (12) Sholing Girls' School

HEART OF GOLD

My love is like a heart of gold,
I'd keep for you forever to hold.
But now you've thrown my love away,
I cannot live another day.

Sitting alone with all my sorrows,
Still waiting for you to return
I cannot wait until tomorrow
Wondering when my love shall burn.

You do not know the pain I feel
You do not know what you have done
If you come home my heart will heal
And we can remember all the fun.

The days we sat beside the shore
I thought our love would last much more
But now you've thrown my love away
I cannot live another day.

Emmalene O'Sullivan (14) Sholing Girls' School

MY ODE

My sister's out shopping
My dad's cooking tea
My brother's washing his hair
And my mum's helping me.

My other sister's are working
Their children are complaining about school
And my nan's knitting a plain old
Boring shawl.

Gemma House (11) Sholing Girls' School

WORRY AND TERROR OF FOX LIFE

The mother is in her den protecting her cubs
But outside there are men clenching clubs.
The cubs are crying the vixen is scared
And down the hole the big dog glared.
The cubs are hungry they can't get food
All the men are angry and raging in a mood.
The father is making his way home
But little did he know the big dog did roam.
The vixen is scared and it's becoming night
But the dogs and men are wanting to fight.
The father's coming home he is quite close by now
But took one step back as the big dog did howl.
He ran and ran to reach the mother
And all the cubs the men did smother.
As the mother got caught by the ear
Off her nose slipped one little tear.
Then the father finally reached her
He saw blood on her head all over her fur.
The vixen lived but the dog dropped dead
And his last barks were never said.
The foxes left and were very brief
Went into the distance and left in grief.

Sarah Warren (14) Sholing Girls' School

SCHOOL

School is great
School is fun
We even get to make rock buns.

The teachers are alright
And they don't like us to fight!
And when we do they make us turn blue.

I like doing PE
But I hate RE
School is great
School is fun
We even get to make sponge.

Ann-Marie Hickman (13) Sholing Girls' School

HOW TO EAT SPAGHETTI BOLOGNESE!

Try eating it with chop sticks,
Or sucking through a straw,
Don't eat it with your fingers,
It'll end up on the floor!

Try eating it with teaspoons
Or with a knife and fork
But these two eating instruments
Are better used for pork!

Try eating it with tweezers
Or with a cocktail stick
Which one of these would you chose
Make up your mind, be quick!

Joanne Cater (12) Sholing Girls' School

KITTY CAT ANTICS

A little striped ball of fur
Running around the room
Chasing anything that moves
Even the garden broom.
Eating all the chicken that was left from
Last night's tea,
And when I looked into the fridge there was
Nothing left for me.
Putting paw prints on the wall, never thought
It would do this at all.
Chasing all the wool about when granny's
Doing her knitting,
Taking giblets in the garden and throwing them
About.
My naughty little black striped kitten
I don't know what I'd do without you.

Hayley Bevis (11) Sholing Girls' School

DOLPHINS

Swimming here, swimming there
Swimming round everywhere.

Dolphins high,
Dolphins low,
Dolphins in the ocean everywhere I go.

They like to play in the
Water all day
What a wonderful sight
To watch dolphins at night.

Jody Kenway (14) Sholing Girls' School

MAYBE MY HEAD WILL POP!

I wish that I could paint, the sparkle of a star,
I wish that I could buy, the whole of planet Mars,
I wish that sometimes, maybe,
That somebody would tell me, that some day I'll do one
Of these things.

Sometimes in my dreams, I do some funny things,
I play with my toes, some instruments with strings,
I see a crocodile and an alligator smile,
When they're usually doing their toes with a file.

These are just some of the things going round my head
My brother Fred,
Says some day my head will go pop!
If I think anything more I will surely go flop.

Marion Ballard (11) Sholing Girls' School

MY KILLER RABBIT

My rabbit, she is glossy black,
Sometimes if it's been a bad day,
She grunts at me fiercely
Her ears prick up,
When I scream and leg it!
She makes me a nervous wreck,
Nobody believes me of course,
Such an innocent cute little face,
Such a dainty fluffy bob tail,
Whenever I put her outside
She goes and hides behind the shed,
It can take ages to get her back
Why can't she be like all the other rabbits?
So gentle and good natured.

Karen Warrington (11) Sholing Girls' School

BIG ANIMALS AND LITTLE ANIMALS

Big animals and little animals,
There are all kinds of them.
Fat ones, skinny ones,
Tiny ones and huge.
There are hairy ones and scary ones,
And some that have no hair.
Big ones you can ride on them
And ride them like a horse.
Some of them have horrible smells
And you cannot stand it for a minute.
Some animals like cats think they can sleep anywhere,
And they land upon your head,
So you get them off, and you tell them off
And they all go out the room.

Donna Lane (11) Sholing Girls' School

BLACK OUT

In the little house
We all sat in the dark
Thinking about when the world was going
To be lit by a spark.

In our little house we sat
Nobody to see
The dim light of the candle shone free.

Now in our little house
We think about how it would be
To live in light
And be free.

Erica Andrews (13) Sholing Girls' School

THE FUNFAIR

I enter the funfair through silvery gates,
This is the fair that nobody hates,
Spooky ghost trains and funhouses too,
Guaranteed to frighten the life out of you.

If you're hungry, need a snack,
There's something the fair won't lack,
Buy candy-floss on a stick,
Buy sausage rolls and take your pick.

Aeroplanes with flashing lights,
Big wheels get to dazzling heights,
Screams and giggling everywhere,
Horror rails shoot through the air.

Now the fair is filled with silence,
No more pushing, no more violence,
This little fair is now closed down,
Gone on to another town.

Gillian Lye (11) Sholing Girls' School

GREEN

Green is the colour
Of leaves on the trees.

Green is the colour
Of grass swaying in the breeze.

Green is everywhere,
Everywhere you look,
You even find the colour in a book.

Emma Dodge (13) Sholing Girls' School

173

FAMILY CHRISTMAS

We all get together,
Gather round the Christmas tree,
And see what we got each other.

Then Lee shouts, 'Hey it's snowing'
So we all rush to the window,
And white snow is glowing.

We have a big turkey dinner,
With sprouts, peas and carrots too,
And we get fatter, but no thinner.

Then there's a scream from the hall,
It's just the kids playing tag
Because Jessica has just caught Paul.

Then mum says 'Let's go and do some singing,'
Then we sit there and sing
But I say watch Gladiators, see who's winning.

We send the little ones to bed,
And we see what's on the telly,
Oh it's that brill film Drop Dead Fred.

That's how we spend
Our family Christmas
Right till the end.

Nicola King (13) Sholing Girls' School

RACISM

Racism, I don't agree with
It hurts,
It's painful
It's not very pleasant.

Would you like it if it was you?
No, I didn't think so.
I wish everyone would be able to get along
People should by now, be able to smile at each other
Free to live,
In peace, love and harmony
If people could only be happy not sad.

It shouldn't matter what colour your skin is,
Or your language is,
It isn't what you are, it's who you are!

Sarah Lieb (13) Sholing Girls' School

MY FAMILY ODE

I live in a house which is cluttered, and there are always mutters,
Most about social stuff the other about school stuff.

My brother is in the bathroom my dad is on the loo,
My mum goes so fast you would think she flew.

I am just so private you wouldn't know I'm there,
But when I shout they all stop and stare.

Kathryn Smurthwaite (11) Sholing Girls' School

SMILE

Some people say it's funny,
Some people say it's sad,
You do it when it's sunny,
And when the weather's bad.

It makes more people kinder,
They enjoy feeling good,
It's passed on from one another,
Just like it should.

It makes you show your dimples,
It wrinkles up your nose,
It's a thing that's just so simple,
It's a smile, didn't you know!

Joanne Tonner (13) Sholing Girls' School

SPOTLIGHT

My life
When I was one I sucked my thumb
When I was two I got some shoes
Then I was three and I grazed my knees
When I was four I could open doors
When I was five I learnt to dive
When I was six I learnt new tricks
Then I was seven and nearer to eleven
When I was eight I opened a gate
When I was nine the chocolates were mine
Then I was ten I got a hen
When I was eleven I went to Devon
Now I'm twelve I'm really cool
Doing it all at Sholing School.

Joanne Ellis (12) Sholing Girls' School

ODE TO MY BABYHOOD

Memories of long gone days
Lots of time to learn and play
Listening to mummy's story telling
Dirty nappies, always smelling
Hoping for cuddles
And maybe a smile
Nobody's picked me up for a while.

Waiting for daddy to pick up my rabbit
I threw it about, 'twas an awful habit
Feeling warm and secure
Asleep at night with teddy bear.
I've still got that teddy, he's very old
He remembers the day that story was told.

Danielle Naulin (12) Sholing Girls' School

MUM TELL ME WHY

Yellow is the colour of the sand
Green is the colour of the land
Blue is the colour of its eyes
Why do we kill them mum tell me why?

Is red the blood that's on the hunter's hands,
As riffles shoot across their lovely lands.

Why do they do it, it upsets me so,
Why do they do it mum, I don't know.

Laura Carter (13) Sholing Girls' School

ODE TO MY BABYHOOD

Vomit, dribble and dirty nappies,
None of these made me happy.
Freshly bathed with a smiley face,
No-one else could take my place.
They picked me up when I was crawling,
Little did they know
I'd soon be walking!

Jodene Payne (12) Sholing Girls' School

CAGED

Every morning I could hear him sing
but some days he would scream.
It used to frighten me
he was scared.

He would jump
and try to be free.
He was trapped, ensnared,
but still he would sing.

And then he was gone,
it was over, he was silent.
He laid there limp and frail
he was frightened no more.

I could hear crying
but there were no tears,
he had no tears,
he was cold.

Maxine Dawkins (15) Sholing Girls' School

CHRISTMAS

Christmas is a time for fun,
With lots of presents for everyone.
Girls and boys sitting under the tree,
Opening their presents as happy as can be.
The snow outside is falling on the ground,
But inside our house there is laughter all around.
Christmas is a time for family and friends
With cards and presents they send.
You can see from the childrens' faces that
They are happy in their places and they
Never want this day to end.

Leanne Pearce (13) Sholing Girls' School

BIRD OF PREY

Love is like a bird of prey
It hits you from behind
At first it may seem beautiful
But remember love is blind.

The sweet taste of perfection
Will quickly turn away
For after every encounter
Is the cold reality of day.

Affairs of the heart remember
Are like the pages of a book
Everything may be clear
But take a second look.

Even love has its boundaries
So don't step over the line
'Cause if you make a little mistake
It will last throughout all time.

Georgina Macey (16) Sholing Girls' School

MY QUIET CORNER

There's a quiet corner in my room,
Where there is no night or day,
There, time is at a standstill,
I can wish the world away.

I think about a lot of things,
In the quiet corner of my room,
It's a place where I can be alone,
And feel the emptiness, without you.

There's so many things I should have said,
How I wish I'd said goodbye,
In a quiet corner of my room,
I sit alone and cry.

Why can't you come and comfort me?
A little prayer I'll make,
In the quiet corner of my room,
My heart begins to break.

I see an image in the dark,
In the quiet corner of my room,
I'm not on my own, for someone's near,
I sense the presence of you.

You know I'll always love you,
That alone is true,
In my quiet corner of my room,
I'll sit and remember you.

Amy Beard (15) Sholing Girls' School

LISA

When I'm confused and in need of a friend,
She is the only one I can turn to,
In times of trouble when I am alone and afraid,
She helps me and sees me through.

She's the one that keeps all my secrets,
And senses all my anxiety and fears,
She knows what makes me smile and laugh,
And what brings me sadness and tears.

Together we plan for the future,
And share all our thoughts and dreams,
We'll face the world together,
Immortal, or so it seems.

This poem is dedicated to her,
That one special best friend,
With her, life is worth living,
And I'll love her till the end.

Marie Neale (15) Sholing Girls' School

MEMORIES

You held me in your arms,
The memories swirling around us,
We stood together oblivious
of the world that was around us.

Why did you have to leave me?
I knew you really cared
For the precious time and laughter
together we had shared.

And as we stood there silent,
our last few moments together,
I realised that I loved you
and would remember you forever.

So, our time together ended,
we left our separate ways,
I know our time together
will remain with me, always.

Bonny Clayton (15) Sholing Girls' School

SPLINTERED SOUL

The darkness creeps into the room,
A layer of silence, creates the tomb,
The silent screams pervade my head,
The echoing cries of those long dead.

A casualty of success it seems,
Defeated by others' hopes and dreams,
Betrayed by those who I called friends,
A broken bond that never mends.

Sunlight streams onto the floor,
Its warm caress I feel no more,
Cold and dark, my shattered mind,
Among its pieces, my pain you'll find.

A stain of wine, a broken glass,
The anger which will never pass,
My body slumped amongst it all,
Listening to temptation's call.

Unleashing feelings of guilt and hate,
Apologies came much too late,
Demons feeding on the fear,
Not letting others come too near.

The decision was made, to end my life,
Confusion and pain, fear and strife,
Another chosen, I'm left in the cold,
Left to leave, be forgotten, grow old.

Welcoming death, I raise the blade,
Preferring to die than to fade,
A delicate cut no surgeon could mend,
The rush of red, marks the end.

Kathryn Whinney (14) Sholing Girls' School

THE ENEMY

Please mend the damage you have done,
We fought the battle and now you've won.
The lines you threw
To cut in two
Worked oh so well
But now please tell
Are you happier with the enemy
Now that I have set you free?
The golden band
Upon your hand
Like young wives
With sharpened knives
Is my greatest enemy
That must set you apart from me.

Kerry Webb (15) Sholing Girls' School

I WONDER

I wonder how people feel,
when they break up or
lose a loved one.
I wonder how they feel!

I wonder what they're thinking,
I wonder what they do,
I wonder who they talk to,
When they're feeling blue.

Emma Purkiss (13) Sholing Girls' School

CONFUSED

I feel cheated
Why me?
I love you
You are my friend
My best friend.

Yet you hurt me
You lie to me
You promise, I believe
And you deceive.

I know you have a life
Your life, not mine
But why promise?
Why me?

I feel cheated
You were hurt
You are hurt
You have a right to fight
I am confused.

I get angry, I cry
I am hurt, I cry
I feel second best, I cry
Do you love him more than me?

Now what? Where now?
Are you going to make a change?
A permanent change,
Or do I have to remain confused?
Or will I always be confused?

Kelly Jacqueline Paddick (16) Sholing Girls' School

WHAT IS LOVE?

Love is something special,
Love is something unique,
Love is all around,
When two hearts can meet.

Love cannot be brought,
Love cannot be sold,
When you fall in love,
Your heart will turn to gold.

Love can last forever,
Love will never die,
When your heart is broken,
Your eyes can't help but cry.

Love is from your heart,
Deep down inside your soul,
Love will stay inside you,
Love is never dull.

Lauren Hancock (13) Sholing Girls' School

THE OLD MAN FROM YORK

There once was an old man from York,
Who ate his pork with a fork,
He chewed and chewed till he finished his food,
Then went outside to feed his hawk.

Elaine Thomas (13) Sholing Girls' School

THE FOX

Something rustles amongst the leaves,
It pounces,
It jumps,
And away it weaves,
With a mouse in its teeth,
Its head hung low,
Camouflaged against the dark,
Like something long ago.

Something rustles amongst the leaves,
The barrel of a gun,
Away the beast runs,
Startled to panicky flight,
A flash of red,
It stops to rest,
Knowing the hunters are beaten again,
Surely it was the fox.

Emma Male (13) Sholing Girls' School

MY DOG BEN

Me and my dog Ben,
have a very secret den.
We walk there side by side,
and there we go to talk and hide.

We sit and dream the whole day through,
it's lovely and peaceful just us two.
Then we walk home to have some tea,
I love him so much my doggy and me.

Kerry O'Brien (13) Sholing Girls' School

JOURNEY'S END

The war has just ended,
I am laid on the floor,
My leg can't be mended,
It's full of blood and gore.

My friends are all dead,
I am here all alone,
I wish someone would find me,
I want to go home.

It's getting very dark now,
It's getting very cold,
I just wish I had someone,
That I could love and hold.

I see a helicopter,
With light that shines on me,
I pray that it has come to collect,
Little injured me.

As the helicopter landed,
I was told to hold on tight,
The men attached the ropes and chains,
And pulled with all their might.

I am safely back at camp,
With a plaster on my leg,
I know that I'll never forget,
The night I will always dread.

Katie Chant (14) Sholing Girls' School

THE MOST EMBARRASSING MOMENT

I had the most embarrassing moment
When I went out to tea
My skirt got caught in my knickers
Oh no, this couldn't be.

I was half way up the street
When someone called to me
'Eh, look lovey,' he said,
'There's a lot that I can see.'

Emma Parkes (13) Sholing Girls' School

THE WITCH

I thought I saw a witch today
Flying on her broom,
She flew in through the window
And buzzed around the room.

She whizzed down the stairs
And whirled round the hall
Circled round the kitchen
And then she had a fall.

She landed in a messy heap
All scrunched up on the floor
I asked her if she was OK
She said, 'I won't do that no more.'

Joanne Smith (13) Sholing Girls' School

LIFE OR DEATH?

At that moment in time,
When life is coming to an end,
Do we have warning, can we be ready ?
Have we given love, when love has been needed?
Have we been true when doubts have been upon us?

The shadows are darkening like autumn evening,
After the brightness of full summer,
Peace is looming as a voice begins to call,
Drifting now, into a very bright light,
Can this be heaven, or can this be hell?

Heavenly bodies beckon me, but should I really go?

Emma Harley (15) Sholing Girls' School

THE COWARDLY SOLDIER

It's 1939,
And war is on the way,
The bells are ready to chime,
It will come any day.

Soldiers are ready to fight,
They are waiting in position,
On search every night,
For the opposition.

Silence tonight,
They wait, ready to go,
Soon comes a bloody fight,
They have to keep low.

The fight is near,
And people are dead,
But I am here,
Hiding instead.

Joanna Webb (14) Sholing Girls' School

MISERY

I saw you there
Standing cold in the shadows
The tears filled your eyes with sorrow
And the night air chilled your body.

You stood there motionless
Did not know how to move
You were frightened of the world you were in
And what life had in store for you.

The anxiety of life crept upon you
You only heard what you wanted to
Didn't pay attention to the distance of the world
Had you missed out on happiness?

You looked destitute and miserable
Was there a part of you that was missing
Did you find your inner self that night
Your life was not worth living.

You stood helpless, alone
Did anyone care?
The moonlit sky shone upon your face
The cold and the darkness magnified your love.

You kept screaming but no-one heard
You liked the sound of your voice but no-one's listening
You're my friend of misery
The rain just fell as the night faded on.

Joanna Gransden (15) Sholing Girls' School

MEMORIES

Some are good,
Some are bad,
Some will even drive you mad.

Some memories are sad and make you cry,
As time goes by and by.

But time after time,
Those memories come back,
And remind you of the love that you lack.

Shana Brewer (13) Sholing Girls' School

LOVE IS!

Love is like a bar of chocolate,
It doesn't last long
but you can always get another.

Love is like a boomerang,
You throw it away
it comes back and hits you in the face.

Love is like a flower,
It grows, it blossoms
and then it dies.

Love is like a fire,
You light it,
it goes out and you're left to clean up the ashes.

Sarah Hewitt (13) Sholing Girls' School

FEELINGS

I was in such a grumpy mood,
Because my Mum wouldn't give me any food.
I shouted and screamed,
Until she gave me some ice-cream.

I am sat in the corner all alone,
Listening to my Mum on the phone.
She never ever listens to me,
Because she wishes I was a he.

Oh I've got butterflies in my tummy,
How on earth will I tell my Mummy?
I've got a detention after school,
Oh aren't I such a fool.

Happiness is a really great thing,
People shout, dance and sing.
I don't know what I'd do if it went away.
Would I be sad? Would I be gay?

Elaine Thomas & Lindsay Flounders (13) Sholing Girls' School

THE MATHS TEACHER

We have a very strange Maths teacher,
He has very small beady eyes,
He's always on about fractions,
Subtracting, dividing and PI.

He hunches over his table,
Upon his face an evil glare,
Another hour left to go,
So for now we're going nowhere.

Then at the end of the lesson,
We get out our homework diaries,
Five pages, one hundred questions,
He says, 'Hand it in tomorrow, please.'

So now the lesson has finished,
We're finally freed from prison,
We're not really happy because
We have science for next lesson!

Rachael Harley (13) Sholing Girls' School

LIFE!

Life lies ahead,
Life isn't dead,
Life is alive,
Life doesn't thrive,
Until you make it happen!

If you make it happen
This world won't seem that sad,
If you make it happen
It won't be so bad!

Kirsty Maunder (13) Sholing Girls' School

GRANDMA'S POT OF TOMATO KETCHUP

Grandma's pot of tomato ketchup
Ain't what it appears.
Made in 1983
It's had its better years.

Around the rim there is a seal,
Not of glass or plastic
But of sticky ketchup gunge,
Scientifically drastic.

The sauce itself is green and yellow,
And fluff outlines the lid,
And when you hold it to the light
It illuminates the dog.

Helen Poulten (14) Sholing Girls' School

RINGING LOVE

I rang him last night
and I rang the night before
the answer I got was
there's no love anymore.

I rang him again
and the day after that
I wish he hadn't said
our love had gone flat.

But still I rang
but still there was no answer
the bloomin' fool
had changed his number.

Natalie Terry (14) Sholing Girls' School

195

I LOVE HIM, I LOVE HIM NOT

I love him so much,
The way he talks and walks.
The way he smiles and acts.
I love his eyes and hair,
I love him so much.

I hate him so much,
We broke up.
He was with someone else.
I hate everything about him.
I hate him so much.

I love him so much,
We got back together.
He is so sweet, it was just a misunderstanding.
I love everything about him.
I love him so much.

Sarah Clancy (13) Sholing Girls' School

TRICK OR TREAT

I love going trick or treating,
To see what nice people give me to eat
Sometimes I'm lucky
They give me a sweet
Sometimes I'm not, they give me nout to eat.

Karlie Portlock (14) Sholing Girls' School

CHRISTMAS

Wow, it's Christmas the tree is standing tall,
And all around is presents all around the floor,
Some are for my sister and some are for my mum,
But most of them are for me from my auntie, my mum, my nan,
Christmas is such a joyful time, happy too,
Just see your face when you get the present I give you,
And when mum has cooked the dinner,
The turkey, carrots, peas,
I scoff it down in one go and fall down on my knees,
And then I set down in the chair and
Force down some Christmas pudding,
Even though I know I shouldn't,
Then Christmas is over and the happiness has gone,
But in my mind I still remember the
Christmas when we had fun.

Jane Meacher (14) Sholing Girls' School

ESSAY

I'm sitting here,
Bored out of my mind,
Trying to think what to write,
I'm stuck for words,
I'm out of time -
Who cares?
I'll do it tonight.

What shall I write?
When shall I write it?
How shall I write it too?
It's got to be handed in in five minutes
Oh - what shall I do?

Toni Davies (13) Sholing Girls' School

MISSING

A face appears on the screen,
Another missing person who hasn't been seen.

Frantic families searching in vain,
Everybody watching can feel their pain.

A body has been found in the lake,
Could this be the one to make their heart break?

What a relief, not this time,
Now the parents are accused of a crime.

Being accused of killing their son,
This is nobody's idea of fun.

The doorbell rings, a man stands there,
Holding their son with such care.

Silent tears fall from his eyes,
To his parents, it is a surprise.

Hugs and kisses will come soon,
But now he's safe in his room.

Jennifer Skinner (14) Sholing Girls' School

THE UNTOUCHABLE

The untouchable
the one you want
can't have
can't touch
wouldn't dare.

Tall figure
towards you he walks
your heart races
his just beats
no change.

He talks
you absorb his words
every detail
every stutter
you respond but your words fail.

He leaves
you cry
he doesn't know
how can he know
your pain.

The untouchable
the one you want
can't have
can't touch
is gone.

Samantha Johnson (15) Sholing Girls' School

WHEN I GROW UP I WANT TO BE . . .

When I grow up I want to be,
A tree,
Or am I copying that advert on TV.

Maybe I'll be a pilot,
And fly around the world,
Nah, who would look after my budgie.

On second thoughts, I'll be a nurse
Maybe not,
Blood and gore,
I'll be heading for the door.

Maybe a policewoman and stroll along the street
No, I'll get cold feet,
I could be a detective
Like that woman on TV
Maybe not she got shot
Didn't she.

I've decided I'll wait until I'm older
Then I'll decide what I want to be.

Julie Emery (12) Sholing Girls' School

PEOPLE

People come in shapes and sizes,
Some are tall and some are small.
Some are loud, they scream and shout,
Some are quiet without a doubt.

You can make friends with some,
A best friend can be lots of fun.
You may have similar interests like,
Swimming, running, riding a bike.

When you get older girls also like,
Meeting boys and going out at night.
Some boys can grow up very quick,
Some can turn out actually quite thick.

Parents can also be quite a bore,
They don't let you out of the door.
If this happens you all start to fight,
It's not often a very pretty sight.

Lorraine Graham (12) Sholing Girls' School

JUST LIKE THAT

He's perked up my smile just like that,
He's melted my heart just like that,
He's filled up my dreams just like that,
and it's all because I love him.

He's saddened my smile just like that,
He's broken my heart just like that,
He's shattered my dreams just like that,
and it's all because I loved him.

Amanda Owen (13) Sholing Girls' School

THE KNICKER-BOCKER-GLORY

There it is standing on the table,
So innocently,
Waiting . . .
Just waiting for me!

I get a spoon,
I delve straight in,
All the frothy cream on top,
Delicious.

I'm down to the bottom now,
I don't feel too good,
Oh! Why did I eat it,
Right, that's it! No more knicker-bocker-glories ever.
I promise!

Well . . . maybe one day I'll have another one.

Charlotte Turner (12) Sholing Girls' School

HOW WE TREAT THIS WORLD

This morning,
I went outside and I sat down
And I listened to what I could hear,
Birds singing a tune,
Watching all the flowers bloom,
Then I heard a monstrous sound
Of cars and lorries going round and round,
If we treat the world like this,
Would we live, forever, 'I wish.'

Kelly Jenkins (13) Sholing Girls' School

THE SHOPPING TRIP!

Mum comes strolling in the room
She picks me up.
'Come on we're going shopping'
'Oh no, not shopping, mum.'

Out the door, into the car,
She straps me in,
There's no escape,
We're on the road, 'Oh no.'

We're in the supermarket
What a bore,
'Mum please hurry up,'
I'm dying here, 'Come on let's go.'
We're in the sweets section,
'We can go now love,' she says
'Not now mum please.'

Sally Cartwright (13) Sholing Girls' School

THE WORLD'S MY PLACE

This is my world,
the world's my place.
Look at me,
look at my face.

Am I happy,
am I sad.
Look at me,
I'm very glad.

This is my world,
the world's my place.
Look at me,
look at my face.

Caren Crimble (12) Sholing Girls' School

THE SPIDER

Crawling, seeking behind the cider
Sits a big, fat, juicy spider.

The spider that I see is sly
Waiting for a tasty fly.

He waits and waits all day and night
But not one fly comes into sight.

My mother sees him sitting there
And goes screaming up the stairs.

My dad comes in and squashes him flat
And slides the dead spider under the mat.

Bonny Donnarumma (13) Sholing Girls' School

CHRISTMAS MORNING

I rush down the stairs on Christmas morning,
The birds are singing and the cat is yawning,
The first thing I do is run to the tree,
And look to see if there's a present for me.

I find one there, 'Yippee' I say,
Oh this has been a wonderful day,
I open it up, wow, it's a pair of socks,
'Thanks mum you've made my day.'

Katie O'Grady (12) Sholing Girls' School

KOALA BEAR

Brown and fluffy
Black and white
Koala bears are a beautiful sight.

Soft and cuddly
Two little eyes
Big, black nose
And fluffy toes.

Little baby koala
On its mother's back
Wandering in the trees
And eating eucalyptus leaves.

Saundrine Allcock (12) Sholing Girls' School

TWIN SISTER

I have a twin sister
who looks like me
when I have my tea
my mum never knows what one's me.

When we watch TV
my mum brings us tea
my sister flicks the peas and blames it one me
why me mum, please, why me?

When I have a cup of tea
my mum shouts at me
for spilling my tea
but by then I have no tea.

Michelle Diaper (13) Sholing Girls' School

THE WORLD'S ANIMALS

Dolphins swimming in the sea,
Birds singing in the trees,
Cats squabbling,
Dogs barking,
Bees buzzing,
Parrots peeking,
We have all of these.

Debbie Godfray (13) Sholing Girls' School

CHRISTMAS DAY

I walk down the stairs to the Christmas tree,
I see a present,
What could it be,
Is it for him, her or me?
Oh, someone tell me,
What could it be?

I walk up the stairs,
With it tightly in my hand,
Could it be a musical band?
Or could it lead to a foreign land?

I put my hand on top of the box,
Could it be a wild fox?
No-one knows,
No-one knows,
Except for I,
And I alone.

Natasha Dunster (13) Sholing Girls' School

MY MUM

My mum shouts at me all day long
but I don't know what has gone wrong.
You naughty girl, what have you done.
I don't know, honestly mum.
She's like this all day long but I have
not done anything wrong.

Joanne Whitehead (12) Sholing Girls' School

MY HAUNTED HOUSE

Creepy, spooky
And all dark
I was in my room
When I saw a spark
As I looked closer
It was a fire
I told my mum
But she thought I was a liar.

But that night as I was
Lying in bed,
I heard a noise,
So I turned round my sleepy head
And there it was, a blobby thing
Come from the dead
And it started to sing.

Run away if you dare
But wherever you go
I'll be there.

Charlene Doughty (13) Sholing Girls' School

MONSTER NONSENSE

My monster is from space,
He's the last of his race.

He's green,
He's supreme.

He likes to talk,
He does a funny walk.

He likes the boys,
Mainly because of their toys.

He's like a pet,
So I take him to the local vet.

He tells the vet
That he's my pet.

He's got a fat belly,
He's got a fat welly.

He's got a strange head,
Guess what . . . it's red.

He's very funny,
He's got some money.

Now that is the end of my
Verse.

Kay Boyce (13) Sholing Girls' School

MY LITTLE BADGER

I have a little badger,
he sleeps in my bed,
It's not really a badger,
it's a puppet instead,
He wakes up in the morning,
he opens his eyes,
Then I think,
he's really real inside,
Then he gets dressed,
has a little play,
Then I think,
it's another day.

Mandy Woolnough (12) Sholing Girls' School

CHRISTMAS DAY

Christmas day is almost here
I can hardly wait
I can't get to sleep
Although it's really late.

It's Christmas day, I hope it's fun
I can see the rising sun
The rising sun means it's time
Time to see what I can find.

I found my presents
I've found my sack
Apples, oranges
A selection pack.

Christmas day was here and gone
I can't wait until next year
I can see snow falling
Happiness I can hear.

Virginia Richardson (13) Sholing Girls' School

THE SEA

As I watch the sea,
Splashing up at me,
Shining in the sun.

As I watch the sea,
The waves,
Jumping, flying free.

As I watch the sea,
As I watch the waves fly,
I give them a wave goodbye.

Helen Burchell (13) Sholing Girls' School

WEATHER

When you get up in the morning,
The sun shines in your room,
It looks like a beautiful morning,
And everything's going your way.

Then when you arrive at school,
It starts to pour with rain,
You're so upset and miserable,
Like something has affected your brain.

Then when you're ready to go,
It starts to thunder and snow,
You're so frightened,
You try to hide,
Then you fall and hurt your side.

Kelly Willmott (13) Sholing Girls' School

THE CHASE

Quiet and peaceful as the sun rises,
Then a quick ripple as the trout comes up, followed by a large pike.
Down the river they go until they see a waterfall in front,
And then down and down until,
Splash, they are down.
The trout knows he has got a chance.
So a long swim up and a jump.
The trout has made it and he swims off.

Natalie Bedford (12) Sholing Girls' School

MUMMY'S LITTLE SOLDIER

Mummy's little soldier
Is a little boy who creeps
He can't do a thing wrong,
Or so our mother thinks.

He eats all the biscuits,
And hides all the sweets
Just because our older sister
Wants her midnight treats.

Mummy's little soldier
Is her little honey bun,
No matter what he does
He's still her favourite son.

Hayley Brindley (13) Sholing Girls' School

I WISH

I wish I was a million miles away
As far as I can go
Around the world to Africa
I wish, I wish, I could go up to space to Mars or Jupiter
And visit the moon.
Just to get away from this place,
I wish, I wish, I wish I could do these things
Up I could go.

Michelle Randell (12) Sholing Girls' School

BLACKY THE CAT

Dark as night
Light as day
Then my cat goes out to play
Up a tree round and round
She jumps off then hits the ground
With a bird in her mouth.
Mm yum, yum
It's my tea
Pigeons pie that's for me
Swirling down
Mm yummy, yummy
Not it fills up my tummy
What's for pudding?
Bluebird pie
It's so lovely I could die
What's for tea tomorrow I wonder?

Annette Le Moignan (12) Sholing Girls' School

MY FAVOURITE SEASONS

Winter
Winter is cold and breezy
Building snowmen is nice and easy.

Snowballs flying past the doors
Smashing windows is the laws.

Christmas is coming soon
Look Santa's flying over the moon.

Christmas morning you wake up and see
Lots of presents under the tree.

Spring is nearly here,
All the snow is nearly clear.

Winter is fun but not in all its ways,
Oh all those happy winter days.

Spring
Spring is full of brightness
Lots and lots of lightness.

Huge amounts of flowers everywhere,
Smell of blossom in the air.

Gardens full of bright green grass
Children in their summer clothes walking past.

Sun is going in, out comes the moon.

Older children thinking I don't want to
Go to bed it will be morning soon.

Sarah Brine (11) Sholing Girls' School

TRUST

You trusted me, I trusted you,
But what did you do and do?
You told my secret to everyone,
Because you thought it would be fun,
When it all got back to me,
I was upset as you can see,
I thought our friendship was based on trust,
But you went and told, you thought you must.

Emma Chapman (13) Sholing Girls' School

MY RABBIT

I have a rabbit
Who looks like a faggot
He's so light
Because he's white.

His name is Snowy
People call him Chloe
I tell them no
His name is Snowy not Chloe.

He lives in a cage
People call it a rage
In it he has straw
With lots more.

Kerry Jefford (12) Sholing Girls' School

BOYS

Boys, boys
They're nothing but trouble
Us girls are the best
At least we don't get a hairy chest.
Sometimes I hate them
Sometimes I like them
But most of the time I kiss them
All the boys, come up to play
Most boys are good looking anyway.

Kailey Milne (12) Sholing Girls' School

HELIX

Helix is a punk
He always gets so drunk
He sometimes goes to the pub
For his daily grub.

Helix has yellow hair
Nothing like a teddy bear
Walking around everywhere
In his T-shirt a great big tear.
Out at night
On his bright new bike.

Kristal Jerrim (12) Sholing Girls' School

WALLPAPER

Wallpaper on the wall
On someone's school books, some not at all.
Some are screwed up on the floor,
Who knows where paper goes.
Some down in cracks, some down your pants,
Some in clamps or may be eating gnats
Or flats who knows where wallpaper goes.

Emily D'Arcy (12) Sholing Girls' School

A VERY GOOD FRIEND

My good friend is very nice to me,
She buys me presents and comes over for tea.
But she sometimes calls me names
And jokes at my expense and that's why I say
Friendship doesn't make much sense.

We've been friends a long time,
Through first and middle school,
I went to New Zealand one time
She came twice to Blackpool.

It's not very fair, is it?
How she lives her life with it
And I live mine without,
I guess money's not important though,
At least I've been about.

Sarah Eccles (13) Sholing Girls' School

THE EASEL OF EMOTIONS

Red is for anger, rage and despair,
Yellow is for brightness, happiness and cheer,
Pink is for candy-floss, love and delight,
Black is for the dark that we see at night.

Blue is for ice, water and wind,
Green is for envy which you just can't keep in,
Purple is for fun, magic and wonder,
White is for peace, purity and surrender.

Lucy Summerfield (14) Sholing Girls' School

HOW LONG HAVE I KNOWN YOU?

How long have I known you?
7 years, that's how long.

We should have got together then
But we were both too shy, busy, pre-occupied.

But now, I've realised the error of my
Ways and I also realised I've loved
You from the moment we first met.

You admitted you loved me in year 3
And I turned you away. You came to
Me crying, 'Why had I let you go?' Of
Course, I regret that now.

And it breaks my soul when I think about it.

I wish we could be together but your
Life and my life have taken separate
Paths, but please take me back to the past.

Adele Cann (13) Sholing Girls' School

MIDNIGHT FEAST

Mum baked a chocolate cake today
I wonder if it's still there,
I suppose there's no harm in looking
It's not like I'm going to eat it is it?
I'd better be quiet
Mum's a very light sleeper.

Oh! I forgot about the cat
He insists on sleeping at the bottom of the stairs,
Silence
Now to find the kitchen
It must be here somewhere
Ah, here it is,
Complete with chocolate cake
Chocolate icing
Chocolate strands
Chocolate cake!

There's a piece missing
Must have been dad,
Do you think they will notice?
Do you think they will be mad?
If I just took the tiniest minute piece,
Well, we'll soon find out in the morning
I'll just cut it here
Oh, whoops! The knife has slipped
They're sure to notice now!

Claire Shergold (13) Sholing Girls' School

THE THIRD WORLD

Flies are flying,
Children are crying,
People are dying,
We are sighing.

The children sit here,
Their lives full of fear,
Do you or I care
That their bodies are bare?

Their parents are dead
Not owning a bed
Lie flat on the ground
Maybe never to be found.

Left to live alone,
Without food or home
Do you or I care
About the state of their hair?

Children just sitting
Screaming and crying
Unable to move
For they have no food.

They freeze at night
Maybe loose their sight
Does anyone care
That they have no clothes to wear?

This place of sorrow
Maybe the world of tomorrow
Show you care,
Or give some clothes
For them to wear.

Natalie Brenton (13) Sholing Girls' School

BLACK AND WHITE!

Black is the colour of the night,
And also the colour of fright,
It is the colour of sorrow,
That will still be here tomorrow.

It is the colour of the soil,
And of thick, shiny oil,
It is the colour of sticky tar,
Which stretches out so far.

In contrast there is white,
Which is the opposite to fright,
It represents peace,
And the christening of someone's niece.

White is the colour of a ghost,
Who scares me more than most,
It is the colour of the stars,
Which shine all the way to Mars.

Helen Green (13) Sholing Girls' School

THE GREAT SPAGHETTI RACE!

When my friend suggested that we both have a race,
I was all for it, I was full of charm and grace,
But when she said spaghetti, I cracked up on the floor,
She gave me a really dirty look and headed for the door,
The very next week I went to her house,
The spaghetti in bowls on the table,
It really looked unappetising, just like rolled up cable,
Oh, but even thinking about it makes me feel really sick,
I had to eat three bowls of it, what a lousy trick!

Katherine Crouch (11) Sholing Girls' School

THE LONER

She sits in the corner all alone, all alone,
No-one loved her so she left home,
Her clothes all tattered, her lips turning blue,
I bet she wishes she could start anew.

She looks up, as a stranger passes by,
And says in a weak and fragile voice,
'Please sir, could you spare me
A couple of pence for a cup of tea?'
He walks on by, not saying a word
And pretends as if he hadn't heard.

As the stranger, walks out of sight,
She thinks of what his home might be like,
Warm and cosy with lights all around
Fresh food on the table, his family around.

She shivers in the freezing cold,
Around her are others, both young and old,
Her eyes all watery, she starts to weep,
And slowly, slowly, falls asleep.

Shakira Tengnah (13) Sholing Girls' School

KILLING

Why do people do it,
Tell me this please.
What makes people be
So stupid and seize
Poor innocent people's lives.
When they have done
Nothing wrong?
I wish I could understand why
Killing is so wrong.

Rebecca Horrocks (12) Sholing Girls' School

MY ONLY FRIEND

My only friend
Is not quite a friend
But he is the only one I've got,
He's small but fat
His mum is big but thin.

I love him like my own son
We sit together in the sun
We sit under the stars
We sit and look at the moon
I wonder why.

My friend cares for me
And I love him to
He looks after me and
Loves me.

His name is Ted and
Guess who he is
He is a teddy bear
But I love him.

Tina Louise Gardner (11) Sholing Girls' School

MY BROTHER DAN

My brother Dan
Is a travelling man
He's twenty three
And much bigger than me.
He's been to Africa
He's been to Greece,
He wants to save the rhino
And help to keep the peace.
He likes to play his music
He likes to ride his bike,
He'd ride it across the desert
But he wouldn't take a hike.
He wants to save the animals
He wants to set them free
He wants to keep them safe
For kids like you and me.

Jennifer Cooke (11) Sholing Girls' School

MY MUM SAYS ...

My mum says I must eat greens,
Like cabbage, sprouts and broad beans.

My dad says I must eat,
Potatoes, carrots, baked beans and meat.

But I prefer
Pizzas, McDonalds and chips.

I love fudge, candy floss, chocolate and
Treats, but they all rot my teeth.

Helen Gardiner (12) Sholing Girls' School

SEASONS

Winter
Winter is my favourite season,
Snow falls to the ground,
November, December, January,
No-one is around.

Spring
All the blossom buds in spring
Daffodils are yellow,
We go and play amongst the dew
Then the cattle bellow.

Summer
Summer can be very hot
Sometimes very cold,
Summer is my mum's birthday
She is not very old.

Autumn
In autumn the trees undress
They are very bare
All the leaves fall to the ground
And children play there.

Teegan Mist (11) Sholing Girls' School

POLLUTION

Poison gases pollute our sky,
Oil slicks cover all our seas,
Lead fumes dull our brains,
Leaves, brown and shrivelled, flutter to the ground,
Unchecked, it will kill our world and us.
Time to do something before it is too late.
International help is needed,
Oceans need cleaning,
Not a moment to lose.

Emma Warriss (13) Sholing Girls' School

A DEVOTED FAN

I've got their posters above my bed,
Their latest song buzzes in my head,
Their pictures are plastered all over my wall,
Their names are written on my books for school.

I sit and think of them all day,
They are on my mind, and that's where they'll stay,
At disco's I drive the DJ mad,
He thinks that their music is totally sad.

My favourite T-shirt bears their name,
Their music drives my dad insane,
I daydream of them during my school classes,
I will love them . . . until this obsession passes.

Jenni Stokes (14) Sholing Girls' School

NIGHT TIME

Night time is a special time,
When the sky is full of magic things to see.
When the moon is full and the stars are out
The owls are hooting in the trees.
The sky is purple and blue never black or dull at all.
Flower buds close all over the land in gardens all around.
Sun sets at seven and darkness falls upon us all.

Lisa Turner (11) Sholing Girls' School

AUTUMN

I sit upon a park bench listening to the wind,
The golden brown leaves rustle in the breeze,
The smell of damp grass and the fresh soil,
Watching children throwing leaves and playing conkers.

The falling of helicopters twirling like
Catherine wheels and the thudding of horse
Chestnuts dropping from the trees.
The mist was rising and the air was clear,
The wind was getting stronger so I started to walk home.

I passed some people burning leaves
And children collecting firewood, with rosehip
                                        noses,
As I walked through the woods,
The sun sparkled through the trees,
And the frost glistened on the grass
I was under the spell of autumn
And the only way out was to wait
Until winter.

Rachel Orchard (13) Sholing Girls' School

MY JOURNEY TO THE UNKNOWN

It happened about two weeks ago,
I was sleeping, dreaming I was in space.
The unknown,
I was in this spaceship
Dressed in a silver spacesuit.
With a glass helmet on.
I was surrounded by green skinned aliens,
Dressed in yellowy, brown capes,
With purple boots on.
They had a funny way of communicating,
They were talking in a
Kind of a screeching noise.
They were panicking,
Running around.
I asked what was wrong,
They didn't understand.
Then a big purple skinned alien came
Out of nowhere.
He understood English very well
Because he understood my words,
What's wrong?
He said 'Please drive us back to the planet Zog'
I said 'Yes' and he showed me how to drive the
Spaceship.
10 seconds later we were there.
He explained the real captain had got ill and
Couldn't concentrate, to drive us home.
He said something but I couldn't make out what.
Then I woke up, sweating a bit,
I wonder what will happen tomorrow night?

Anna Lebbern (12) Sholing Girls' School

MY DREADED SCHOOL REPORT

Today was the day my school report came,
I knew I had only myself to blame,
I couldn't help messing around,
Or making a very loud sound.
Or putting a frog in my teacher's tea,
He deserved it after what he said to me.
You don't concentrate or try your best,
And don't even bother when you have a test.
He ranted and raved and shouted things,
Until my ears started to ring.
Now it's come to the crunch,
I was pleased to go out to lunch,
Now it is the afternoon,
Home time is coming soon.
My dad met me at the door,
And I just looked at the floor
What's the matter my girl he said
You look flushed maybe you should be in bed,
I handed him the report, I felt all cold,
The envelope he started to unfold.
What's this he said as he read through the pages
A good report the first in ages.

Clare Jarvis (14) Sholing Girls' School

GETTING SCARED

I wonder if he'll shout at me,
I'm having him soon I'll have to see.
I wonder if he'll blow his top,
And I'll have to hold him down to make him stop.
I bet you that he'll rant and rage,
And make me tear out the entire page.
He always talks for ages and ages,
By the time he's finished I could have written pages,
They say that his dad is a preacher,
But I shouldn't be scared as I am the teacher.

Laura Hills (13) Sholing Girls' School

KITTEN

Our cat, Misty has had her kittens,
As I looked at them I was smitten.
Small round balls wrapped in fluff,
They looked so innocent, but I knew they were tough!
For when I put out my hand to smooth their backs,
A kitten bared its claws, I was under attack,
A throbbing scratch, a huge big gash,
Then it was over quick as a flash,
I glared at her as if I didn't care,
But the monster that wounded me wasn't there,
Instead all that was left in its place,
Was a tiny smooth kitten with a beautiful face.

Angela Grinsell (13) Sholing Girls' School

MY MEMORIES

The memories between you and me,
Are something lost we can't see.
I still remember
We were good friends of each other,
We often sang together
Always studied with cheer,
We made fun of each other,
But never faced trouble with fear.
Now no laughter's are left in the air,
Your footprints disappear,
Just remaining your empty chair,
But my memories still appear.
The tears fall from my eyes,
As I stand beneath the blue sky.
Why does the time pass and hide?
We can't catch it though we try.
Please don't answer with hesitation.
Can you come back quickly?
Don't leave me again quietly.
You are my real friend
Our friendship will never end.
Please keep our memories preciously
And memorises thoughtfully.

Ivy Chan (14) Sholing Girls' School

WHALES

Whales swim in the sea,
They move through the water easily,
Whales spout water high in the sky,
People kill them I don't know why
They do no harm to you or me
So why can't people let them be.

Sara Burden (13) Sholing Girls' School

AN ELEPHANT

An elephant arrived for tea,
What a surprise.
'Who asked him? It wasn't me.'
He was grey and fat looking at me,
I thought for a second.
'Shall I let him in?'
Oh yes but . . . how would he get in
I walked away leaving the door open
I looked around
He got through the window
I gave him a cup of tea
He drank it in glee
It took six seats to seat him all
I offered him a sandwich
He said 'Six please.'
I gave them to him.
I said, 'Are you on your way now?'
'Of course I am.'
'How are you getting out?'
'The way I came in.'
'Okay then,' so off he went.

Sarah Ballard (13) Sholing Girls' School

THE DECEPTION OF THE SEA

The sea like a mirror reflects the sun's light,
First shades of jade, turquoise then white,
The sea appears quiet, serene and still,
While under its currents, it's preparing to kill.
The surface is peaceful, gentle and calm,
While secretly plotting to do you harm.
Finally succumb to the charm of the sea,
You step aboard boat to realise the fee
The sea turns wild as it rages and roars,
Waves just get higher as upward they soar.
Now they come crashing dashing the boat,
While crew members struggle to stay up afloat.
After the storm has subsided and gone,
And birds back to singing their melodious song,
All wreckage is washed, washed to the shore,
The horrible nightmare can't be heard anymore.
As the sun disappears, sinks into the sea,
All that is left is the wreckage and me
The sun going down brightens your life,
As the sunset's colours soak up your strife.
Streaks of fire red fill up the sky
Crimsons and ambers across the skyline fly
Tomorrow will be fine, it's red sky at night,
You know how the rhyme goes, shepherds' delight
You're caught by the beauty, stand there in awe,
Waves no longer crashing, they no longer roar.

Sarah Payne (15) Sholing Girls' School

WORKING SHOW

Stop that noise,
Give me a break,
I need some rest,
Not a big headache,
I've been working all day,
I don't need all this,
I've just got in,
Now give me a kiss,
Today I saw the boss,
He said I work very hard,
Do you want some chips,
Now where's the lard?
He showed me how to type,
He said I learned quick,
Suzy got jealous
And gave me a kick.
Now we've eaten tea,
It's of to bed we go
I'll see you tomorrow
For the same working show.

Elizabeth Owen (16) Sholing Girls' School

LOVE

Love is here
Love is there
So what am I doing here?
I often wonder to myself
What is above the clouds?
Maybe there is a love
Waiting for me
And one day I shall see!

Emma Stuart (14) Sholing Girls' School

HOW CAN THIS BE FAIR?

My perfect grandmother was once there for me,
No matter what I had done.
She laughed and smiled once with glee,
Then suddenly she had gone.

I sit alone in a room,
Wondering what we did.
Happy times only loom,
Since I'm just a kid.

The pain of loss I feel inside,
No-one seems to care.
I seem to let the pain just hide,
How can this be fair?

Amanda Jerrim (14) Sholing Girls' School

WINTER TIME

Seeing the snow on the ground,
The happy faces all around,
Running, jumping in the snow,
In their wellies as they go.

Throwing snowballs at each other
Hit me and then another.

Wet and soggy out to play all day.

Our mums call us for tea
But we're still playing happily.

The day's gone by really quick, we're
Coming out tomorrow if we're not sick.

Gemma Elrick (11) Sholing Girls' School

6 STAGES OF MODERN WOMEN

Time to get up
Always in a rush
Changing smelly nappies
Getting bottle warmed up.

Start to crawl
And making a mess
Screaming and yelling
For a hug.

Time to get up
You must not be late
Go play with your friends
And be back before it gets late.

Start to see the world
Not knowing where to go
Having lots of fun
Facing the future all a glow.

Time to settle down
Have a baby or two
See them grow up
And see me grow old.

Start to get wrinkles
As another day goes by
Wondering what to do next
So much to do before I die.

Claire Pinckney (15) Sholing Girls' School

THAT DREADFUL DAY

They did not believe me until that day,
That my parents had passed away,
My nan and grandad came to school,
Then we all gathered in the hall.
First to speak was grandad,
When he spoke I felt sad,
He said my parents had died in a car accident,
They were coming home from Kent,
It was my birthday that day,
When my parents passed away,
My sister was only three,
I heard the news and she cuddled me,
I had one question to ask, why?
Why oh why did my parents die?
For my birthday gift that day,
My parents passed away.
The news was like stabbing me with a knife,
But everyone said I have to get on with my life
The last five years have gone fast,
But I will never forget the past.

Gemma Davis (14) Sholing Girls' School

WINTER SNOW

Winter's near come and play,
Get your gloves out today,
Go and get your sleigh to play,
We'll play until it fades away,
Now we're off we can not stay,
Now it's time to dream the day away.

It's morning time the sun appears,
The snow melts like a tear,
Let's get dressed before the snow
Gets near,
Let's go out and see if the snow
Is still there.

Lucy Randall (11) Sholing Girls' School

LUCKY THE RABBIT

I like to stroke his smooth, brown hair
I walk towards him,
His ears stand on end
Sometimes
If you're very quiet,
You can see him washing himself gracefully.
He sits there
Staring at you
Nibbling away
On a piece of carrot
He thinks about his interesting rabbit life.

Verity Harding (11) The Atherley School

ARES, MY CAT

A sleek black body,
Cleaning his coat,
Till it is perfect.
If I bat an eyelid,
He will pounce on me,
As if I were a mouse.
He lies completely still,
Except for the occasional
Twitch of an ear,
Sunning himself on my lap.
I run my hand down his back,
His fur feels like silk
Under my fingers.
He begins to purr
In contentment:
Then pushes his paws
Into my lap.
To show he's happy.
With long flowing movements,
He rises and crosses the room.
I can see the muscles,
That help him run and pounce
So gracefully:
Filled with pent up energy.

Carmel Stock (11) The Atherley School

MY CAT

In the house, my cat
Is a comfortable creature
Purring like an old man snoring
On my bed
At peace with the world
He pads
Round the room
Like a child wearing velvet slippers.

Outside, a different story
A would-be tiger
Chasing his tail and dead leaves
Sitting on a tree
Claws unsheathed
Like a hunter with his gun at the ready.

Olivia Fennell (12) The Atherley School

A MOTORWAY

A motorway is like a long, long snake,
White line patterns over its back,
It is a giant conveyor belt,
Carrying goods,
A messenger courier,
Full of messages,
Like a person,
Alive with business,
A tiny galaxy,
In the middle
Of nowhere,
It is like a brain.

Elizabeth Jones (12) The Atherley School

THE OLD MAN

I sit on the bench watching the children play,
They stare at me,
I smile at them,
They ignore me,
I stand up and walk towards them,
Of course they run away.
If only they knew I don't want to hurt them,
I just want to say hello,
But they don't want to know me because I'm old and grey,
Like an old oak tree.
Summer and spring have passed me by,
Winter just around the corner.
But I can still kick a ball,
Run,
Smile,
Laugh,
Have fun.
But as I said before,
They don't want to know me.
So I sit on the bench,
Watching
The children
Play.

Dawne Wakelin (12) The Atherley School

THE MOTORWAY

Like a long line of spaghetti,
the motorway travels
from county to county.
Cars zooming
this way and that.
A column of ants,
scurrying.
Drivers
looking bored.
Children squabble
in the back of cars,
like playful tiger cubs.

Sara Lovell (12) The Atherley School

THE CASHIER

Another tin of baked beans.
Another bottle of orange squash.
I feel all hot and sticky.
I could do with a wash.
It seems like I've been here
Since I don't know when!
Here comes another customer.
Oh, no, not again.

Haley Dyer (13) The Atherley School

MY AUNT

My aunt, Delia Dust,
Wears a farmer's cap,
To beat at dust and dirt.
She wears a sack apron
And a sack shawl
And wellie boots on her feet.

With a bucket and mop,
She dare not stop
Even for coffee at eleven.
In shine or slush
Every step she'll brush
Till the floor gleams like the path to heaven.

With dirt and grime,
Both in and out,
She lovingly cares for her home.
From the front door brass,
To window panes and glass,
In the skylight over the stairs.

In a twizz she'd be,
If her husband came in from the garden
Without treading carefully
On newspaper sheets
Spread over the kitchen floor.

You may think this house,
Too clean for her spouse,
But there's no sorrow nor strife,
Over dirt or dust,
As this husband of hers is equally fussed,
And as good or as bad as his wife.

Jane Haley (14) The Atherley School

242

MY GREAT AUNT

My great aunt was ill.
I didn't know why.
Always in hospitals,
Never in peace.

All I remember
Were hospital beds,
Spotless white sheets
And a strong smell of
Disinfectant.

The view from her window
On a warm summer's day
Was of flowers and meadows,
Only a dream.
But it seemed to relax her.
She would sit for ages
Just gazing, gazing
At what life might have been.

By the time
I was old enough
To understand.
She had escaped.
Escaped from the torment of life.
That, I could not
Understand.

Cathy Thompson (14) The Atherley School

MY GRANDMOTHER

Her favourite place was
the armchair.
She used to sit there
in her lounge
watching people walk past the window.

My grandmother never listened
to anyone.
She blocked herself away
sat patiently
waiting for the grandfather clock
to chime -
every hour.

My grandmother was
pots of tea,
woolly cardigans
armchairs
and knitting needles.

She was frail
quiet
and peaceful.

Now her home is
empty.
The armchair is left
sitting by the window.
The grandfather clock is
chiming
chiming
sadly on its own.

Isabel Ewen (14) The Atherley School

AUTUMN

Tall, slight, middle aged
woman.
Rings school bell,
for summer children.

Laughter fades,
all is still.
One solitary figure,
crossing lonely fields.
All behind her poppies grow.

She comes closer
red cheeks are visible.
Long black hair flowing,
touching trees in the forest.
Bowing humbly they shed their multicoloured leaves,
cushioning her path.

Hard features
visible now.
The small creatures,
frightened,
respect her.
Scuttling to the hibernation
they prepared all year.

Cold face,
walks past telephone wires
birds take flight.
Winging their way to friendlier skies.

Passing me by
one glance, cold as ice.
She mingles with the shadows,
then is gone.

Alexis Blades (13) The Atherley School

THE SEASONS

Summer,
Wearing bright red tulips,
Children,
Wearing colourful,
Summer clothes.

The summer sun,
The glowing of a child's face,
Children's eyes sparkling,
Like the dew on the grass.

Slowly,
The children disappear,
Adults take their place,
This time wearing autumn colours,
Blending with the trees half bare,
The leaves rustle under foot,
Whispering, whispering.

The adults vanish,
An old frail man replacing them,
Walking slowly as if lonely,
Sighing
He freezes the pond.

Soon the spring will emerge
Summer following after.

Nina Chandé (12) The Atherley School

AUTUMN

Autumn is a frail old woman.
The happiness of summer has gone,
Like the happiness of her youth.

Slowly getting colder,
Slowly getting older.

The last leaves fall,
Like the last years of her life.

Jackie Freeston (13) The Atherley School

THE ROLLER COASTER OF LIFE

Life is like a roller coaster.
It goes up,
It goes down.
Some parts are fun,
Some parts are scary.
You go round corners,
You meet new people and new things.
Some parts you love,
Some parts you hate.
And you do love,
And you do hate.
And at the end,
Do you look back on your life with joy,
Happiness and contentment,
Or with sadness, hatred and discontent.
That is for you to decide,
It is your ride, you control it.
So make it a good one.

Melanie Ball (13) The Atherley School

MY BUS DRIVER

Miles and miles he drives
As the same roads pass by.
The same things he sees
Cars, people, trees.

He's like a camera filming
The town.
He studies the streets
Up and down.

Each stop, some people
Enter his bus
Always a bustle
Always a fuss.

As everyone battles
To get off the bus
The bus driver sighs
'Come on what's the rush.'

His eyes look dreary
He's ready to dream.
Only a few more hours
Before he can sleep.

Gemma Murray (13) The Atherley School

I SWEAR BY THE MOON AND THE STARS IN THE SKY

I swear by the moon and the stars in the sky,
All I do each night is pray,
I don't want you to see me cry.

The birds and the bees can fly,
Well it's just another day,
I swear by the moon and the stars in the sky.

I say 'Hi'
Live life to the full in every way,
I don't want you to see me cry.

Open your mind and don't lie,
Get a way,
I swear by the moon and the stars in the sky.

Have a nice day,
I don't want you to see me cry.

I swear by the moon and the stars in the sky,
Save yourself for another day,
I don't want you to see me cry,
The birds and the bees can fly.

Alison Judge (14) The Petersfield School

THE FIRE

The fire grew and grew at the fair,
Then squealed like stoats when bombs began to fly,
The brown land was the colour of hair.

The foul odour floated in the air,
And despair rose like smoke in the sky,
As birds flew away to find a new lair.

Anger was grasped in his hand, like a bear,
Fire, like the moon and stars in the sky,
The fire grew and grew at the fair.

The brown land was the colour of hair,
Screams of fear scared passers by,
The fire grew and grew at the fair.

As enormous bonfires raged like a bear,
The flames grew higher in the sky,
The fire grew and grew at the fair,
The brown land was the colour of hair.

Matthew Farr (14) The Petersfield School

BOX FULL OF DREAMS

'What's that?' said the boy,
as he stood in the hall.
'Just a box' said his mum
from the doorway.
'Can I have it?' He said,
with a smile on his face.
'Of course' said his mum,
'Now run off and play.'

'Just a box' he thought
as he hurtled through space,
in his inter galactic space craft.
He dodged a few meteors
and headed for Mars.
Hitting warp factor nine he laughed:

'Just a box, just a box!
How could grown ups be blind.'
He thought as the engines went zoom.
He shot past Venus
and back towards earth,
crash landing back in his bedroom.

So perhaps it is *just a box*
in literal terms
but to a child -
much more it seems.
Although we see nothing,
there is something there . . .

In a child's box full of dreams.

Mark Child (17) Totton College

POOR OLD FELLA

He seems so smelly,
Tatty torn trousers.
Flat cap and gloves
A bed so hard,
Just a cardboard box.
Pleading for help,
Begging for money.
Unshaved with spots.
Wet with a cold.
Holes in his shoes.
No doctor to see him,
Looking so ill.
Sleeps on the damp streets,
With nothing to eat.
Shouting out messages
'Any old rags?'
'Any old bags?'
His wet damp face
With a long black beard,
Looks so sad,
All alone,
Poor old fella.

Laura Shutt (11) West Wight Middle School

MIRROR GIRL

I stood beside the mirror frame,
Seeing reflections, images the same.

With sparkling glass, like a sunlit prism,
The cracked looking glass concealed the prison.

And as I looked, with a sudden shimmer,
A face I saw, a slight faint glimmer.

A girl with long hair appeared in the mirror,
Her silvery outline gradually grew clearer.

Her lips they moved, but no sound came,
The words were trapped within the frame.

The shiny glass that held her there,
Grew misty as it felt warm air.

The breath of someone, who tried to call,
To speak, to shout, to cry, to bawl.

To scream, to laugh, to yell, to lisp, her
Mouth would try to talk or whisper.

The girl's eyes moved and suddenly,
The mirror split and set her free.

Towards the door, she made her way,
Words on her lips, she could not say.

Across the floor, the girl she glided,
And what then followed is undecided.

I haven't seen that girl anymore,
Whether she's still here, I can't be sure.

But next time into the mirror I gazed,
The smooth, cool surface was cloudy and hazed,

And written on, a message read:

Seven years bad luck.
For though, the words' meaning, to me was a blur,
I had a feeling inside me, that they were from her.

Hayley Briscoe (12) West Wight Middle School

POVERTY GIRL

There she stands
All alone
No-one with her
She's on her own
Those wide asking eyes just stare at me
On a chalk white face there's misery
But why is it like this?
It's really not fair
She needs someone to love her
Someone to care
She has no money
Her feet are bare
She needs someone to love her
Someone to care.

Christine French (12) West Wight Middle School

MIRROR POEM

I went to the fair with 50p clutched in my hand,
And I walked right over to the tombola stand.
I put my hand in the bag, and pulled a ticket out,
Number one hundred and forty eight, I heard the lady shout!
I glanced across the table, to try and find my prize,
And there it was, a golden mirror, right in front of my eyes!
I went back to my home then, that was all for me,
And anyway, I had to go home, it was time for tea.
That night, I looked in my mirror, I wanted to brush my hair,
But instead of my pretty face, there was an evil zombie there
Yes, an evil zombie, with blood coming out of its eyes,
And all from that mirror, that little tombola prize!

Poppy Lewis (11) West Wight Middle School

SHADOWED MIRROR

It was very dull one day
A boy saw a mirror that was thrown away.
He hung it on his bedroom wall,
There was nothing strange at all.
Until one day something occurred,
It was something that he heard
He looked in the mirror on the wall,
A faded figure very tall,
Was standing in this strange mirror
With a lovely kind of shimmer
The boy turned around,
The figure faded in the ground.
The boy began to scream
It was a reoccurring dream
Oh good the boy cried out
He threw the mirror with a shout.

Danielle Oakham (11) West Wight Middle School

255

OLD MAN

He has no friends,
He has no family
He has no house or bed.

He has no money
He has no food
He has no place to rest.

His bed is a cardboard box
His clothes are tatty old rags
His things are in bits and shreds.

Matthew Ellis (11) West Wight Middle School

GRUMP

Tramps, tramps they're all about us,
This one's nice but usually grumpy,
The grass he sleeps on is always lumpy,
He hasn't had a shave in weeks,
And he nearly always weeps because
No-one says 'Here have this for keeps.'

His clothes are ripped and torn,
So he always sticks out,
But he tries to miss out on nout.

Shattered and shambled and sometimes
Rambled, a tramp is the worst type to be!

Joseph Harris (11) West Wight Middle School

INFINITY

Mirrors glimmer shimmer
And shine,
Nine magic mirrors all at one time.

Reflecting infinity all the way round,
Then not even making a sound.

I look in the mirror then the parts fall,
And all around on the walls is infinity reflecting on me.

Lucy Whitham (12) West Wight Middle School

SMOKY

Bright blue eyes
and long straggly hair
lonesome look
and he's nearly bare
one decent meal would be rare
and he loves the open air.
Big black boots
just standing there
happy times long gone and past
lying down to turn in for the night
it's such a shame, such a young life.

Ruth Webber (11) West Wight Middle School

FRED

A scruffy tramp called Fred
With long black hair
He's tired and dirty
It's really not fair.

He's actually that type
That's friendly and kind
He doesn't eat much
Only what he can find.

He begs for money
And scraps of bread
He sleeps in doorways
Lonely, cold, unfed.

Old and weary
No family, no home
No friends to stay with
He's all on his own.

A scruffy tramp called Fred
With long black hair
He's tired and dirty
It's really not fair.

Hannah Church (11) West Wight Middle School

LONELY

He got chucked out about one year ago,
He was all alone with nowhere to go.
He walks up and down in the pouring rain,
Until he gets cold and goes home again.
He's made a few friends, they all call him Phil,
He lost his house when came a large bill.
He didn't have enough money to keep his home
And all he does now is roam alone.

Hollie Blake (11) West Wight Middle School

THE OLD CODGER

An old man limping along
An old man singing a song
An old man who needs someone to care
An old man who had thinning hair
An old man cold and alone
An old man with no thought of home.

Adam Morgan (11) West Wight Middle School

FAR AWAY BEAUTY

I sit at my bedroom window and stare
At you standing right up there,
Landscaped hills stretch far away
I look at you day by day,
You rule the skies for miles around
You live on a hill more than a mound.

Abigail Moore (11) West Wight Middle School

CARDBOARD CITY

Cardboard city is his name,
A stray dog is his friend,
Cup of tea twice a day,
To keep him warm,
His life is so empty,
Due to the love he lost,
Memories of the old days are all he's got.

Becky Sallis (11) West Wight Middle School

ALONE

I am all alone
Out in the cold
No-one's about
They don't hear me shout
I'm freezing and starving
Looking about
To spend the night out
I'll scream once more
The door is opening
They are in
They've seen me
They're letting me in
She said 'Warm milk.'
Oh! How lovely
And my favourite bed
Isn't life wonderful
A warm fire, warm bed and a saucer of milk
Isn't life great
Sleeping on my mat
And being a cat.

Paul Thompson (11) West Wight Middle School

260

A TALL THIN MAN

A tall thin man walked from the mist
A tall thin man that no-one had missed
A tall thin man had forgot how to wish
A tall thin man that once had a home
A tall thin man that is now all alone
A tall thin man was dirty and smelt
A tall thin man wore a leather belt
A tall thin man steals beer and bread
A tall thin man wants to be fed.

Djamel Houfaf (11) West Wight Middle School

FRIENDS

A friend is someone who cares for you,
And someone you can care for too.
Who thinks not only of themselves,
But also thinks of you as well.

A friend is someone who gives advice,
And offers help without asking a price,
Who looks to you for all their faults,
And knows they're always first in your thoughts.

A friend is someone you can trust,
Who will never let you down,
And if you ever need them
Will always be around.

A friend is someone who thinks a lot like you,
On most things except those but a few.
These may cause the occasional row,
But without that you wouldn't know,
What great friends you are now.

Katie Borrill (13) Wildern School

AFTER THE MURDER

No-one seemed quite sure how it happened,
A few people claimed they heard shots,
But weren't so certain when the police pressed for details
Amongst the buzzing spectators, gathered around so fervently.
They whispered, conferred, chatted - Who? How? Why?
Nobody seemed directly interested in him,
He who lay outstretched upon his stony bed,
Covered politely with a white sheet, which was
Blushing before the jostling crowds.

It didn't seem to matter that he was actually dead,
Dead? Just a word (only four letters!)
The police seemed intent on acquiring information:
'When did it happen? Who saw anything?'
The response was minimal.
The real point of interest was being driven off in the wailing ambulance
Then the crowd seemed just to float away.
For their attentions had swayed again.
This time to supper and evening TV.

Yet the Sergeants remained, hovering, seeking evidence.
Except nobody knew anything.
Nobody even wanted to know anything. Not anymore.
The policemen eventually gave up,
And returned, empty handed, to their station.
'Do you really think it was murder?'
'Of course. I can't imagine why such a young . . . ' And bluntly stopped.
Because he could imagine.
And so could everybody else.
So they made themselves a cup of tea,
Turning their attentions elsewhere.
That seemed to work.

Nigel Parsons (15) Wildern School

SECURITY

The mother sits her new born baby in her arms
as she looks into the innocent eyes of the baby,
she turns back time to when she too had lay in
her mother's arms, absorbing the love and warmth.

Judith Furnell (15) Wildern School

STAR OF THE NIGHT

Star of the night,
Shine so bright,
Give me light, light of the night.

Light of the night,
Am I right, give me the light
The light of love, the love of the light
That shines so bright.

Have I got the might to put up a fight
The fight of the might
The fight of the light.

How about a kite
That's not right
The fight of hate, but the kite of sight
So give me the light
The light of flight, sight or love.

Jayne Smith (12) Wildern School

THE LEOPARD

The leopard is a spotty cat
Heavens who has ever seen that?
He prowls about to hunt for food
When nobody can tell his mood.

He lays in wait for something to eat,
An animal that has plenty of meat,
In the long, thin grass he sees a snake,
And thinks what a nice meal that would make.

He leaps towards the look alike worm,
And digs his claws in nice and firm
The snake is stunned because he thought,
That he would never, ever be caught.

The snake struggles to be set free
But the leopard is determined to eat him for tea,
The snake is getting weaker and weaker
Whilst the leopard is making the cuts deeper and deeper.

While the snake struggles to fight for life,
The leopard tears him apart like a knife,
Eventually the snake gives in
And the leopard delightfully starts to dig in.

After enjoying his meal,
The leopard starts to feel
Full of food and in a good mood
And lies down for a snooze.

Lee Stevens (13) Wildern School

DISASTERS OF THE DEEP

Remember back to 1912,
When Titanic roamed the sea?
She hit that great big iceberg,
With no more time to flee.

She might have been unsinkable,
But sink she did without trace,
1000 lives lost, without cause,
Each one and every face.

Safety has moved on from then
And from that fateful day
We think we all control the sea
But no we don't, so pray.

For along comes the Estonia,
Her safety checks all done?
That great big seal upon her doors,
Has gone and come undone!

The water rushes in right now,
It comes in very fast
But the people lie asleep in bed,
Dreaming their very last.

140 people dead,
What a waste of life,
Over 800 missing still,
What a lot of strife!

So just you remember people all
Who think you own the sea.
King Trident is not pleased with you
So be good to him . . . you see!

Alex Plant (12) Wildern School

POOR

When I can't buy what I want I say,
'I really think I'm poor,'
But looking at the world today
I know now I'm not quite sure
What is meant by poor.

Some people haven't enough to eat
They have no chance to choose their life
And cannot stand up on their feet
Sometimes a child has no mother
And a husband has no wife.
I'm beginning to know what is poor.

A rich man has a house and car
And all he wants and asks for
But when suddenly he's hit with a bar
He cannot see as before.
So is he now poor.

He cannot replace his health
However much money he had to spend
So health is better than wealth.
So is being poor and healthy better in the end
Well, it depends on what is poor!

I think I'll try and be
More aware of the fact
That there are a lot of people poorer than me.
So I must not want things I lack,
But thank Allah I'm not poor
But very rich after all.

Zabunnassa Noor (12) Wildern School

I HATE SCHOOL!

School is just so boring.
You have to get up too early in the morning
You eat your breakfast; feel half dead,
Wish you'd stayed in your
Nice, warm bed.

You walk to school, and you arrive late,
Your tutor asks, 'Where have you been?'
You answer sarcastically,
'I have been to see the flippin' queen.'

The teacher says, 'You have got a detention.'
All my thoughts run through my head,
I pretend not to pay any attention,
'Okay' he says, 'You now have three.'
'Fine' I replied, 'Don't worry!
Be happy.'

In the afternoon, I was sent to see the head,
And I said to him, 'I hate this school
And
I would also love to drown
Some of your staff in the
Awful tasting swimming pool.'

I strolled into maths, my teacher starts screaming,
'Get out!'
I replied, 'Okay, calm down, no need to shout!'
At three o'clock the bell rings for the end
Of the day.
Everyone in class shouts
Hooray!

Oh, how I hate school!

David Fox (15) Wildern School

MAN FROM SWANWICK

There once was a man from Swanwick
Who drank quite a lot of tonic.
He came home one day,
His wife said 'Hey!
You'd better have gin with your tonic!'

Sylvia Powell (12) Wildern School

THE GLOW OF CANDLE LIGHT . . .

The glow of a candle,
In the dim cold air,
To give you that feeling
There is peace, somewhere out there.

The coldness of barbed wire
Guarding the flame,
Stopping all peace
Since when war first came.

The stillness of the candle
In the dark, dark night,
Telling the barbed wire
Give up the sorrowful fight.

The coldness of barbed wire,
Slowly fading away,
Letting the flame grow and grow
Giving happiness away . . .

Heather Agnew (13) Wildern School

WATER FROM THE SKY

Pitter patter goes the rain,
Wearing away at the window pane.
It comes in March and April showers,
Drips and droplets fall for hours.

It falls down from the sky,
Like a tear drop from your eye.
Crash, bang, thunder and lightning,
Whistle, hiss, sounds frightening.

But, then out shines the sun
And it sounds like a drum.
Pitter, patter, drip, drop, plop.
Will it ever give up and stop?

Hannah Dudley (12) Wildern School

MUM!

Don't talk to me like that dear,
You will do as you're told!
You're not going out with that on,
You'll wear a coat, it's cold!

Don't waste your money on that thing,
Money doesn't grow on trees!
Did you forget your manners?
I didn't hear a please!

Have you fed the dog dear?
Is all your homework done?
You can guess who talks to me like that,
My lovely darling mum!

Claire Brooker (14) Wildern School